The Age of the Female II

Heroines of the Shift

Richard Andrew King

The Age of the Female II: Heroines of the Shift

The Age of the Female II

Heroines of the Shift

by

Richard Andrew King

Richard King Publications

© by Richard Andrew King
Published by Richard King Publications
PO Box 3621
Laguna Hills, CA 92654

Library of Congress Cataloging-in-Publication Data

King, Richard Andrew
The Age of the Female II: Heroines of the Shift
ISBN: 978-0-931872-04-4

DEDICATION

To my mother, Margaret, whose
strength in the face of adversity
and ability to endure and survive
the most trying of destinies
has made her my personal
Heroine of the Shift.

Acknowledgments

To all those heroines - past, present and future -
who have given a lift to mankind through
their dedication, determination and courage
in pursuit of excellence.

To my good friend, Cristina van Bladel,
furniture designer, artist and earth healer,
for her loving support and encouragement
of this work and its message.

Many thanks, once again, to Shannon Yarbrough
for his wonderful help and cover design.

Richard Andrew King
PO Box 3621
Laguna Hills, CA 92654-3621
www.RichardKing.net

The Age of the Female II
Heroines of the Shift

Table of Contents

King

The Age of the Female II: Heroines of the Shift

INTRODUCTION

This book was a real joy to write. During my research into what I truly believe to be The Age of the Female, I found myself in awe, even sometimes in tears, with what many of the women featured in this book have done with their lives, how they overcame enormous adversities, lived through the oftentimes unkind vicissitudes, challenges and hardships of life and yet triumphed, leaving a legacy of courage, strength, accomplishment and grace in their wake as an unspoken, unsolicited and inspirational gift to all of mankind for ages to come.

The last thousand years of world history were devoted to male energy (Yang) as marked by the number One (1). This next thousand years will be devoted to female energy (Yin) as marked by the number Two (2). The numbers 1 & 2 and their concomitant attributes are diametrically opposed energies, as opposite as any two numbers can possibly be. Planet earth is now smack dab in the middle of a massive shift in the energies of these two opposing millennia, a shift which began on 31 December 1957, and will not conclude until 31 December 2031. "Heroines of the Shift" references some of the females and their accomplishments who have made stellar contributions to the world during this massive shifting of cosmic energies. For more information on this shift, refer to The Age of the Female: A Thousand Years of Yin.

The fact that this new age focuses on Female/Yin energy in no way diminishes men or males. Rather, it allows them to embrace the Yin aspect of life, for all life does have two sides and to focus on one to the exclusion of the other is to deny the reality of what is - a two-sided paradigm of creation where balance is primary and peace rests in the

King

acknowledgment of both day and night, left and right, mind and emotion, male and female.

One book cannot contain all of the achievements of every woman on this earth who has distinguished herself and made valuable contributions to society. Why I chose the women I did is unknown even to me, and I offer my apologies to those courageous and accomplished females who are not featured here, hoping that everyone who reads this work will understand that the women highlighted serve as examples and vanguards for all women and their most noteworthy offerings to life and humanity.

It is also my hope that men will read the excerpts of these women and learn to value them as individuals whose lives and accomplishments transcend gender. After all, we're all made of the same divine substance. We're just housed in different forms, but the form has nothing to do with the basic composition of life as reflected by, but not limited to, qualities of intelligence, courage, determination, creativity, professionalism, leadership, artistry and heart which reside in all of us. It is my wish that everyone on this planet will come to acknowledge, embrace, nurture and support the Yin aspect of life, for without it there could be no life at all.

Richard Andrew King

CHAPTER ONE

YIN RISE

Sun rise, moon rise, Yin rise.

Eyes turn heavenward to skies aglow

with the cresting wave of the cosmic wind

catapulting Yin into ascendance.

No more concealed, her power revealed.

Soaring wings and spreading sails

lift her high where none deny

the presence of her presence.

In every field she wields her force.

In every field her seed is sewn.

Scepter, kingdom, crown and throne

for a thousand years are hers to own.

A warning though from Yang to Yin

to avoid the traps of where he'd been

in his thousand years of going round:

"Uneasy lies the head that wears a crown."

In cosmic time the rise of the Yin was quick. In the eye blink of a hundred years she went from nescience to presence; from obscurity to notoriety; from that which was concealed to that which was revealed. The emerging tsunami of the 2nd Millennium lifted her

King

to skies where all eyes could not ignore her, nor any power deny her, for now *she* had the power and it was and is hers to hold and share and care and dare to wear for a thousand years. But let her be wise, open her eyes, and avoid that which the Yang had found: "Uneasy lies the head that wears a crown." (William Shakespeare: King Henry IV. Part II. Act iii Scene 1)

In viewing the ascent of the female, it is almost comical to think that in the annals of world history she was regarded as the weaker or inferior sex. In some parts of the world she is still considered so. However, nothing could be further from the truth. Ask any woman.

The numerological reason for her former subservient perception was that woman had not come into her own as far as cosmic time was concerned. The last thousand years were clearly dominated by the 1 energy, the energy of the male. In that millennium he and his power were given center stage. He had the floor. It was his words, his actions, his philosophies which ruled and were saluted, acknowledged, indulged, valued and honored. In those times of the 1st Millennium, times which have now passed, Yang had the spotlight. Scepter, kingdom, crown and throne were his to own and his alone.

However, as the energy of the 2nd Millennium approached during the Twentieth Century, female attributes, philosophies and ideals began to emerge. The 2 vibrations of the 2nd Millennium, which are feminine by nature, energized the 2 energy of woman. Hence, she began to emerge as a butterfly from its cocoon. That emerging transformation has now taken place. The ideal of woman has been given a regenerative birth, and it is her essence that will govern, rule and underscore the next thousand years. She now has the floor, and it is her time to take center stage in the glow of the cosmic spotlight and deliver her performance in the great theater of life.

Two notes. The first, as explained in *The Age of the Female: A Thousand Years of Yin* (Volume One), is that the energies of the female are not exclusive to form or gender. They represent vibrations present in both males and females, although they are primarily manifest in females, just as the 1 energy is primarily manifest in males. Both males and females will be dominantly affected by Yin energies for the next thousand years, the positive energies of which will be support, partnership, togetherness, relationship, kindness, caring, courage, tenderness, compassion, balance, fairness, feeling, diplomacy, sensitivity, receptivity, heartfelt emotion, intuition and peace. In its negative aspects, the Yin energies will manifest as adversity, hindrance, interference, contention, confliction, destructive competition, pettiness, duplicity, deceit, overt self-saturation, division, separation, unkindness, coarseness, vulgarity, cowardliness, imbalance, excessive emotion, insensitivity, non-receptivity, irrationality and war.

The negative aspects involve the misuse and abuse of power. As Shakespeare so aptly stated: "Uneasy lies the head that wears a crown," and as Lord Acton commented in a letter to Bishop Mandell Creighton in 1887: "Power tends to corrupt, and absolute power corrupts absolutely. Great men are almost always bad men."

These are disconcerting and sobering statements. They are, as most of us would also agree, true statements. So often the allure of having power is perceived positively; positively that is until one has it and realizes not only its assets but liabilities, responsibilities and dangers. The higher we climb, the harder and potentially lethal the fall. The consequences from taking a fall while we are walking are not so worrisome, dangerous or lethal as that fall experienced from a hundred story skyscraper or a towering precipice. Results from the first are recoverable; results from the second, deadly.

Lord Acton's comment also brings caution and admonition to the possession of power. Power truly does corrupt. It is difficult for anyone upon whom the test of power is placed to remain humble, judicious, equitable and magnanimous in its disposition. Heads easily swell to dangerous proportions when power flows freely through the veins of the empowered. That is, it flows freely until the bubble bursts. Then power is seen for the insidious and dangerous dacoit that it is. Unfortunately, once the fall has taken place, resurgence, reparation and reinstatement of the power is impossible. Once the balloon bursts, the glass breaks, the egg is shattered, all is irreparable and tragically lost.

Acton's phrase that "great men are almost always bad men" certainly is a generic statement embracing all men in the universal sense and is not gender specific. *Men*, in other words, encompasses both male and female genders. In this new age women will have to guard against the abuses of their own power.

During the Age of the Female, women will definitely achieve greatness as never before. And when this occurs, will it then be said that "great women are almost always bad women?" The future holds the answer. The truth is that, as with men, there will be greatly benevolent women and their will also be greatly malevolent women. It might also be worthwhile to recall the words of Nobel Peace Laureate Jane Addams:

The Age of the Female II: Heroines of the Shift

I do not believe that women are better than men. We have not wrecked railroads, nor corrupted legislature, nor done many unholy things that men have done; but then we must remember that we have not had the chance. [1]

Now women will have the chance to prove their mettle. The caution is that for women on the cusp of power, it is better and safer to fall from a pebble than a precipice; to go down in history as a heroin, not a villainess, and to wear a crown that lauds and applauds, not defrauds; that illuminates, not exterminates; that glorifies, not desanctifies and that consecrates, not desecrates.

Female Firsts

That women are powerful, courageous, intelligent, talented, brilliant, artistic, athletic, commanding and gifted is nowhere more visible than in the following catalogue of 'female firsts.' When one reads and realizes the accomplishments of Twentieth Century women and all the positive attributes and characteristics that those attainments reflect, one cannot but reflect upon the intrinsic and inestimable value of the female.

The Twentieth Century, the last one hundred years of the Age of the Male and the concomitant ascent of the Age of the Female, exhibited noteworthy and remarkable achievements by women in all fields of human endeavor. Although not all 'female firsts' could be mentioned in the following list, the ones below have been selected to reflect the rise of the female as she assumes her role in the history of mankind. Furthermore, let it be put to rest, that by reviewing the following catalogue of achievements, women are most assuredly not the weaker sex. It is time for a reality adjustment and a rebalancing of factual perspective.

Yin Rise
Female Firsts of the 20th Century

1900		n/a
1901		n/a
1902	Gertrude Atherton	Writer begins the biographical novel form. American social worker.[2]
	Lillian D. Wald	Organizes the Visiting Nurse Service and the Henry Street Settlement; pioneers the first public school nursing system.[3]
	Martha Washington	The first U.S. woman to appear on a U.S. stamp.[4]
1903		n/a
1904	Mary McLeod Bethune	The first woman to establish a secondary school that later became a 4-year accredited college.[5]
1905		n/a
1906		n/a
1907	Esther Vandeman	The first woman Roman field archaeologist.[6]

1908		n/a
1909	Selma Lagerlof	The first woman to win the Nobel Prize for Literature (Sweden).[7]
	Jane Addams	The first woman president of the National Conference of Charities and Corrections. In 1910 she received the first honorary degree ever awarded to a woman by Yale University.[8] Nobel Peace Laureate, 1931.
1910	Blanche S. Scott	The first woman to fly solo in an airplane.[9]
	Huda Sha'arawi	Organizes and begins the first general-education school for girls in Cairo.[10]
	Madame C.J. Walker	First American self-made millionaire.[11]
1911		n/a
1912	Juliette Low	Founder and first President of the Girl Scouts of the America.[12]
1913		n/a
1914		n/a
1915		n/a

The Age of the Female II: Heroines of the Shift

1916	Sirimavo Ratwatte Dias Bandaranaike	Three times Prime Minister of Sri Lanka; the first woman in the world to hold the office of prime minister. Her daughter later became President, then Prime Minister of Sri Lanka.[13]
1917	Kate Gleason	The first woman to be the president of a US bank. She was also the first woman to be a member of the American Society of Mechanical Engineers.[14]
	Loretta Walsh	The first female Yeoman in the Navy.[15]
1918		n/a
1919	Jeannette Rankin	The first woman to serve in the U.S. Congress; one of the first women in the world to be elected to a major legislative body at a time when women could not even vote in most states of the United States. A lifelong pacifist, she voted against U.S. entry into both World War I and World War II, becoming the only member of Congress to do so.[16]
1920	Ethelda Bleibtrey	The first American woman to ever win an Olympic gold medal. In fact, she won three gold medals during the 1920 Olympic games in Antwerp, Belgium.[17]

	Florence E. Allen	The first female judge.[18]
1921	Bessie Coleman	World's first African-American aviator and the first African-American woman pilot honored with a U.S. Stamp.[19]
	Margaret Gorman	The first Miss America.[20]
	Bessie Coleman	The first African-American licensed as an international pilot.[21]
1922	Lilian Gatlin	The first woman pilot to fly across the U.S.[22]
	Rebecca Felton	At eighty-seven years of age she became the first woman U.S. Senator appointed by the governor of Georgia to fill a vacancy.[23]
1923	Margaret Grace Bondfield	British trade union leader who became the first woman to attain cabinet rank in Great Britain.[24]
1924	Nellie Tayloe Ross	First female governor in Wyoming and the first female governor in United States history.[25]

The Age of the Female II: Heroines of the Shift

	Miriam Ferguson	First female governor of Texas and the second female governor in the United States.(ditto)
1925	Florence R. Sabin	The first woman to be elected to membership in the National Academy of Sciences. She was also the first woman to become a full professor at Johns Hopkins Medical School, and the first woman president of the American Association of Anatomists.[26]
1926	Gertrude Ederle	At nineteen years of age she was the first U.S. woman to swim the English Channel.[27]
1927		n/a
1928	Amelia Earhart	First woman to fly across the Atlantic Ocean.[28]
1929		n/a
1930	Amy Johnson	The first female pilot to fly alone from Britain to Australia, which she achieved at the age of twenty-six. Her flying career began in 1928. Other triumphs included becoming the first female ground engineer licensed by the Air Ministry,

being awarded the C.B.E. for her flying achievements.[29]

1931   Maxine Dunlap   First woman licensed as a glider pilot. [30]

Jane Addams   The first woman to receive the Nobel Peace Prize for founding and managing a settlement house called Hull House in 1889 in the slums of Chicago. A settlement house was a means to mitigate the harsh conditions of poverty found in the cities.[31]

1932   Amelia Earhart   The first woman to fly solo across the Atlantic Ocean, establishing a new record for the crossing: 13 hours and 30 minutes. For this feat she was awarded honors by the American and French governments.[32]

Hattie Wyatt Caraway   On January 12, 1932, Hattie Wyatt Caraway of Arkansas became the first woman ever elected to the United States Senate after winning a special election to fill the remaining months of her husband's term. Arkansans elected Hattie Caraway to the Senate two more times, and she served in the U.S. Senate until January of 1945. In 1943 she became the first woman to take up the gavel on the Senate floor as the Senate's presiding officer.[33]

1933	Frances Perkins	The first woman to hold a cabinet position in the United States - Secretary of Labor - appointed by Franklin D. Roosevelt..[34]
	Nellie Tayloe Ross	The first woman director of the U.S. Mint, serving in that capacity until 1955.[35]
	Ruth Bran Owen	The first woman foreign diplomat for the U.S.[36]
1934	Maureen Catherine Connolly	Known as "Little Mo," she was one of America's greatest female tennis players and the youngest to win the U.S. national singles title (age sixteen). In 1952 and 1953 she successfully defended the U.S. title; she was Wimbledon Champion in 1952, 1953 and 1954; completed a grand slam of the world's four major titles in 1953 with the French and Australian championships.[37]
1935	Amelia Earhart	The first individual (male or female) to fly solo across the Pacific Ocean. Later the same year she set a speed record by flying non-stop from Mexico City to New York City in 14 hours and 19 minutes. [38]

King

1936	Margaret Bourke-White	Photo journalist and writer who shot the cover for the first issue of Life magazine (1936) and her photo essay inside was the first ever published in America. She took the famous photograph of Mahatma Gandhi seated next to his spinning wheel after he made her learn how to spin.[39]
1937	Jacqueline Cochran	Set three major flying records in 1937, and at the time of her death in 1980, held more speed, altitude, and distance records than any other male or female pilot in aviation history. She was also the first woman aviator to break the sound barrier, doing so in 1953 in an F-86 Sabre jet.[40]
	Anne O'Hare McCormick	The first woman to win a Pulitzer Prize in foreign correspondence for her dispatches and feature articles from Europe in 1936. She was a correspondent for the *New York Times*.[41]
1938		n/a
1939		n/a

The Age of the Female II: Heroines of the Shift

1940	Belle Martell	The first female to referee a boxing match.[42]
1941	Annie G. Fox	The first woman to receive the Purple Heart. She died during the attack on Pearl Harbor.[43]
1942	Margaret Bourke-White	The first accredited woman war correspondent.[44]
1943		n/a
1944	Dorothy McElroy Vredenburgh	The first woman appointed secretary of a national political party - the Democratic National Committee. (Alabama).[45]
1945		n/a
1946		n/a
1947	Barbara Washburn	The first woman to climb Mt. McKinley.[46]
1948		n/a
1949		n/a

1950	Gwendolyn Brooks	The first African-American writer to win the Pulitzer Prize.[47]
1951		n/a
1952		n/a
1953	Maureen Connelly	The first woman to achieve a "grand slam" in tennis.[48]
	Jacqueline Cochran	The first woman to break the sound barrier.[49]
	Oveta Culp Hobby	The first Secretary of the U.S. Dept. of Health, Education and Welfare.[50]
1954		n/a
1955		n/a
1956		n/a
1957	Althea Gibson	The first African-American tennis player to win at Wimbledon and was named the Associated Press Female Athlete of the year. She also played with the Harlem Globetrotters and was a professional golfer. Thus, she is one of the greatest all-around female athletes ever.[51]

The Age of the Female II: Heroines of the Shift

1958		n/a
1959	Lorraine Hansberry	The first African-American woman to write a Broadway play.[52]
1960	Wilma Rudolph	At the 1960 Rome Olympics, Rudolph became "the fastest woman in the world" and the first American woman to win three gold medals in one Olympics. She won the 100 and 200 meter races and anchored the U.S. team to victory in the 4 x 100-meter relay, breaking records along the way.[53]
1961		n/a
1962		n/a
1963	Valentina Vladimirovna Tereshkova	Soviet cosmonaut and the first reputed woman in space. She was on the Vostok 5 mission which launched on June 16, 1963, and orbited the Earth 48 times.[54]
1964	Jerrie Mock	The first woman to complete a solo airplane flight around the world.[55]

	Kath Walker	Australian author whose first book, *We Are Going*, a book of poetry, sold out in 3 days. It is the first time an Aborigine had writings published.[56]
1965	Pauli Murray	The first African-American to earn a doctorate at Yale.[57]
	Vivian Malone	The first African-American to graduate from the University of Alabama.[58]
1966		n/a
1967	Muriel Siebert	The first woman to own a seat on the New York Stock Exchange.[59]
1968	Janice Lee York Romary	The first woman to carry the U.S. flag at the Olympic Games.[60]
1969	Shirley Chisholm	The first African-American woman elected to the United States Congress. In 1972, she became the first African-American woman to be a candidate for the Democratic Presidential nomination. She was a nursery school teacher, director of a day-care center and a consultant for the New York Department of Social Services before entering politics. [61]

The Age of the Female II: Heroines of the Shift

	Penny Ann Early	The first woman to play professional basketball.[62]
1970	Anna Mae Hays	The first woman and the first nurse in American military history to attain the rank of Brigadier General.[63]
	Cheryl Brown	Brown, as Miss Iowa, was the first African-American contestant in the Miss America beauty pageant.[64]
1971		n/a
1972	Anne L. Armstrong	A recipient of the Presidential Medal of Freedom, as well as being the first woman from either major party to keynote at a national convention, and the first female United States Ambassador to the United Kingdom, Armstrong was the first U.S. woman to hold a Cabinet-level post - that of Counselor to the President, serving in that capacity in both the Nixon and Ford administrations.[65]
1972	Alene B. Duerk	The first woman to be promoted to the rank of Admiral in the United States Navy.[66]

	Barbara Jordan	A Democrat from Texas, Jordan was the first African-American woman to serve in the U.S. Congress.[67] She was also an advocate for the increased restriction of immigration (Wikipedia).
	Susan Lynn Roley and Joanne E. Pierce	The first female FBI agents.[68]
1973		n/a
1974	Ella Grasso	The first woman elected Governor in her own right (Connecticut).[69]
	Female Episcopal Priests	Eleven women priests were ordained in the Episcopal Church.[70]
1975		n/a
1976	Anne L. Armstrong	The first woman to serve as U.S. ambassador to Great Britain.[71]
	Barbara Walters	Joins Harry Reasoner at the anchor desk of "ABC Evening News," becoming the first woman to anchor a network evening newscast.[72]

The Age of the Female II: Heroines of the Shift

1977	Janet Guthrie	The first woman ever to compete in the Indianapolis 500 (May 1977) and the Daytona 500 (February 1977.) She finished 9th at Indy in 1978 with a team she formed, owned and managed herself. This remains the highest finish by a woman in the Indianapolis 500. She is also the only woman to earn Top-Ten starting positions and post Top-Ten finishes in both of this country's top series, Indy cars and Winston Cup. Until 2002, she was the only woman to earn a starting spot in the Daytona 500.[73]
1978		n/a
1979	Margaret Thatcher	First woman to become Prime Minister of Great Britain.[74]
	Susan B. Anthony Dollar	The first American woman to ever have her image on a U.S. coin.[75]
1980	Roberta Hazard	First woman to command naval training.[76]
	Wilma L. Vaught	The first woman selected for promotion to Brigadier General in the comptroller career field. She was the first General in the United States Air Force.[77]

King

1981	Sandra Day O'Conner	Growing up on her father's cattle ranch in South Eastern Arizona, O'Conner was the first woman to serve on the United States Supreme Court (1981 to 2005).[78]
1982		n/a
1983	Sally Kristen Ride	The first American woman in space - the shuttle Challenger (STS-7).[79]
	Wilma Mankiller	The first woman elected as Deputy Principal Chief for the Cherokee Nation.[80]
1984	Geraldine Ferraro	The first female major party Vice-Presidential candidate (Democratic).[81]
	Joan Benoit Samuelson	Wins the first women's Olympic marathon at the Summer Games in Los Angeles.[82]
1985	Penny Harrington	The first woman police chief of a major city - Portland, Oregon - in January of 1985.[83]
	Libby Riddles	The first woman to win Alaska's Iditarod Dog Sled Race (1,135-miles).[84]

1986	Corazon Aquino	First woman president of the Philippines; TIME Magazine's Woman of the Year in 1986.[85]
	Susan Butcher	Wins her 1st Iditarod Sled Dog Race and goes on to become the only person to ever win the 1,158 mile event three years in a row. She has proven herself as the #1 musher in the world by breaking 9 speed records in major international races. This includes the Iditarod record which she broke by an amazing 31 hours. She is the first and only person to take a dog team to the summit of Mt. McKinley (North Americas highest peak - 20,230 ft.).[86]
	Christa McAuliffe	First woman citizen passenger on a space mission, the ill-fated Challenger Space Shuttle, which exploded a few minutes after takeoff on January 28, 1986.[87]
1987	Wilma Mankiller	The first woman chief of the Oklahoma Cherokee Indian nation.[88]
1988	Susan Estrich	Lawyer, professor and author, Estrich was the first woman to head a national Presidential campaign (Democratic).[89]

King

	Barbara C. Harris	Elected the first woman Episcopal bishop (Massachusetts).[90]
1989		n/a
1990	Captain Marsha Evans	The first woman to command a Naval Station.[91]
	Rosemary Mariner	The first woman to assume command of an aviation squadron.[92]
	Darlene Waskra	The first woman to command a U.S. Navy ship - the U.S.S. Opportune.[93]
1991	Gertrude Elion	The first woman inducted into the National Inventors Hall of Fame.[94]
1992	Mae Jemison	The first African-American female in space during a joint U.S./Japanese science mission.[95]
1993	Janet Reno	The first female U.S. Attorney General (appointed by President Clinton).[96]
	Julie Krone	The first woman to win a Triple Crown race; the first woman to win the riding title at a major track (1987), and the first woman honored in Thoroughbred racing's national Hall of Fame (2000).[97]

The Age of the Female II: Heroines of the Shift

1994	Shannon Faulkner	The first woman to attend the all-male Citadel, a military training institute.[98]
1995		n/a
1996	Sara Deal	The first woman Marine Corps pilot. She was African American.[99]
1997	Madeleine Albright	The first woman Secretary of State and the highest-ranking woman in the U.S. government.[100]
1998	Eileen Marie Collins	U.S.A.F. Lt. Col. The first woman ever selected to be a space shuttle pilot and the first woman to command a space shuttle.[101]
	Kathy E. Thomas	A Vietnam veteran and advocate for the advancement of women, Thomas is the first female Brigadier General in Air Force Space Command -- Reserve or active duty.[102]
1999		n/a

The Age of the Female II: Heroines of the Shift

CHAPTER TWO

NOBEL YIN

Noble,

Nobel Yin -

Women in reception

of accolades and honors

in Physiology and Medicine,

Physics, Chemistry, Peace and Literature -

Bright lights lighting a world with thought advancing,

hearts embracing, hopes emerging, actions leading onward.

Leaders, guides and models all, standing tall amidst the crowd

and offering flames of excellence without a thought of mediocrity.

The Nobel Prize

The Nobel Prize is the first international award given yearly since 1901 for achievements in physics, chemistry, medicine, literature and peace. The prize consists of a medal, a personal diploma, and a prize amount. In 1968, the Sveriges Riksbank (Bank of Sweden) instituted the Prize in Economic Sciences in memory of Alfred Nobel, founder of the Nobel Prize.

In the beginning, more than three prize winners could share a Nobel Prize, although this was never practiced. Paragraph four of the

King

Statutes of the Nobel Foundation was amended in 1968, restricting the number of prize winners to only three. Previously, a person could be awarded a prize posthumously if the nomination was made before February 1 of the same year. Since 1974, the Prize may only go to a deceased person who has been named as prize winner for the year (usually in October) but who dies before the Prize Award Ceremony on December 10." [103]

Alfred Nobel - The Man

Contentment is the only real wealth.
Alfred Nobel

Born in 1833 in Stockholm, Sweden, to a family of engineers, Alfred Nobel grew up in Russia, studied chemistry and technology in France and the United States and became an inventor, technological researcher, entrepreneur and a lover of poetry and drama. In 1866, Nobel invented dynamite as one of the 350 patents bearing his name. His business empire consisted of companies and laboratories in more than twenty countries worldwide. He died of a cerebral hemorrhage in his home in San Remo, Italy on 10 December 1896.[104]

The disposal of his fortune was a considerable concern for Nobel. Before his death on 10 December 1896, he issued his final will and testament at the Swedish-Norwegian Club in Paris on 27 November 1895. In his will he declares:

The whole of my remaining realizable estate shall be
dealt with in the following way: the capital, invested in

safe securities by my executors, shall constitute a fund, the interest on which shall be annually distributed in the form of prizes to those who, during the preceding year, shall have conferred the greatest benefit on mankind. The said, interest shall be divided into five equal parts, which shall be apportioned as follows: one part to the person who shall have made the most important discovery or invention within the field of physics; one part to the person who shall have made the most important chemical discovery or improvement; one part to the person who shall have made the most important discovery within the domain of physiology or medicine; one part to the person who shall have produced in the field of literature the most outstanding work in an ideal direction; and one part to the person who shall have done the most or the best work for fraternity between nations, for the abolition or reduction of standing armies and for the holding and promotion of peace congresses. The prizes for physics and chemistry shall be awarded by the Swedish Academy of Sciences; that for physiology or medical works by the Karolinska Institute in Stockholm; that for literature by the Academy in Stockholm, and that for champions of peace by a committee of five persons to be elected by the Norwegian Storting. It is my express wish that in awarding the prizes no consideration be given to the nationality of the candidates, but that the most worthy shall receive the prize, whether he be Scandinavian or not. [105]

King

Nobel Prize Statistics

The Prizes, as designated in the will of Alfred Nobel, are in Physics, Chemistry, Physiology or Medicine, Literature and Peace. Only once during these years has a prize been added - a Memorial Prize - the Prize in Economic Sciences in Memory of Alfred Nobel, donated by the Bank of Sweden to celebrate its tercentenary in 1968. The Board of Directors later decided to keep the original five prizes intact and not to give permission to more additions. There have been 696 total prizes from 1901 to 2002 in the basic five categories designated in Nobel's will.[106]

Female Nobel Prize Laureates

During *Yin Rise* in the Twentieth Century, women made tremendous advances in all areas of life. Their influence was also felt in the distinguished world of the Nobel Prize. In the years from 1903 to 1997, 29 women were awarded 30 Nobel Prizes spanning all five categories: Physics-2; Chemistry-3; Physiology & Medicine-6; Literature-9; Peace-10. Madam Curie was the only woman to win two Nobel Prizes: one for Physics in 1903 and the other for Chemistry in 1911. The chronology of Twentieth Century Nobel Yin is below, followed by a brief synopsis of the life and accomplishments of each recipient.

Nobel Yin
Female Nobel Prize Laureates
Chronology[107]

No.	Year	Recipient	Category
1	1903	Marie Sklodowska Curie	Physics
2	1905	Baroness Bertha von Suttner	Peace
3	1909	Selma Ottilia Lovisa Lagerlof	Literature
4	1911	Marie Sklodowska Curie	Chemistry
5	1926	Grazia Deledda	Literature
6	1928	Sigrid Undset	Literature
7	1931	Jane Addams	Peace
8	1935	Irene Joliot-Curie	Chemistry
9	1938	Pearl S. Buck	Literature
10	1945	Gabriela Mistral	Literature
11	1946	Emily Greene Balch	Peace
12	1947	Gerty Radnitz Cori	Physiology Medicine
13	1963	Maria Goeppert Mayer	Physics
14	1964	Dorothy Crowfoot Hodgkin	Chemistry
15	1966	Nelly Sachs	Literature
16	1976	Betty Williams	Peace
17	1976	Mairead Corrigan	Peace
18	1977	Rosalyn Sussman Yalow	Physiology Medicine
19	1979	Mother Teresa	Peace
20	1982	Alva Myrdal	Peace

King

21	1983	Barbara McClintock	Physiology Medicine
22	1986	Rita Levi-Montalcini	Physiology Medicine
23	1988	Gertrude Elion	Physiology Medicine
24	1991	Aung San Suu Kyi	Peace
25	1991	Nadine Gordimer	Literature
26	1992	Rigoberta Menchu Tum	Peace
27	1993	Toni Morrison	Literature
28	1995	Christiane Nusslein-Volhard	Physiology Medicine
29	1996	Wislawa Szymborska	Literature
30	1997	Jody Williams	Peace

The Age of the Female II: Heroines of the Shift

Female Nobel Laureates

Twentieth Century

Chronological History

Madam Curie

Nobel Prize - Physics

1903

In recognition of the extraordinary services they have

rendered by their joint researches on the radiation

phenomena discovered by Professor Henri Becquerel.

(Co-recipient - husband, Pierre)

Nobel Prize - Chemistry

1911

In recognition of her services to the advancement

of chemistry by the discovery of the elements

radium and polonium, by the isolation of radium

and the study of the nature and compounds

of this remarkable element.

One never notices what has been done;

one can only see what remains to be done.

Madam Curie[108]

Born in Warsaw, Poland, on 7 November 1867, Maria Sklodowska would become one of the most famous scientists in the world and certainly one of the most distinguished women of the Twentieth

King

44

Century. She was not only the first woman to win a Nobel prize (Chemistry -1903), she was also the first person to win two Nobel Prizes, the second for Physics in 1911.

Growing up in a family that valued education, she traveled to Paris to study mathematics, chemistry and physics at the Sorbonne in 1891. It was there that she adopted the French spelling of her name (Marie). It was also in Paris that she met and married Pierre Curie, a physics instructor at the University of Paris. Teaming up to conduct research on radioactive substances, they discovered two highly radioactive elements - 'radium' and 'polonium.' For this discovery they were co-recipients of the Nobel Prize for Physics in 1903 with Antoine Henri Bacquerel, another French physicist who had discovered natural radioactivity. Unfortunately, weakened by prolonged exposure to radiation, as well as being overworked, Pierre Curie was killed as the result of being run over by a horse-drawn wagon.

Continuing her work, Madame Curie went on to win her second Nobel Prize, this time for chemistry in 1911 for isolating radium and studying its chemical properties. She helped found the Radium Institute of Paris in 1914 and invented X-ray vans to locate bullets in wounded soldiers and to facilitate surgery during World War I. [109]

Madam Curie is notable for many firsts. Among them are:
- 1st woman to win a Nobel Prize for Physics
- 1st person to win a second and unprecedented Nobel Prize
- 1st to use the term radioactivity
- 1st woman in Europe to receive her doctorate of science

- 1st female professor at the Sorbonne University in Paris [110]

Madame Curie died of leukemia on 4 July 1934, at the age of 67. Her death was believed to have been generated by exposure to the high levels of radiation involved in her research.[111]

Baroness Bertha Sophie Felicita Von Suttner

Nobel Prize - Peace

1905

Writer

Hon. President Permanent International

Peace Bureau, Berne

Author "Lay Down Your Arms"

Born on 9 June 1843, Countess Kinsky, later to become Baroness Bertha Sophie Felicita Von Suttner, was the product of an aristocratic society and a family with militaristic traditions, the daughter of a field marshal and granddaughter of a cavalry captain.

The young countess studied languages and music in her youth, maintained an active social life, traveled and read passionately. In 1873 at the age of thirty, she took a position in Vienna as a teacher-companion to the four daughters of the Suttner household. She later married Baron Arthur Gundaccar von Suttner, the family's youngest son. The Suttner family disapproved of the marriage and the couple moved to the Caucasus.

King

The Baroness began to write poetry, novels and a book of serious thought entitled <u>Inventarium einer Seele</u> (Inventory of a Soul). It was in this work that she and her husband discussed authors of the day such as Darwin and Spencer, as well as advancing the concept that society would achieve progress through achieving peace.

As her life progressed, she continued to write novels and eventually became interested in the peace movement of the day. Her novel, <u>Die Waffennieder</u> (Lay Down Your Arms) offered an implied indictment of militarism and made quite an impact on the reading public. From this moment forward, Bertha von Suttner became an active leader of the peace movement and devoted a great deal of her writing, time and energy to it. She attended meetings and international congresses and spoke all over the world to promote peace. She also communicated with Alfred Nobel, informing him of the progress of the peace movement. He informed her of a peace prize he was hoping to create. After his death in 1896, his will confirmed that he had done just that.

Bertha Von Suttner continued to work for peace after her beloved husband died in 1902. Her message, delivered through arduous speaking tours, was one of the oneness of Europe, stating that uniting it was the only way to prevent an ostensible world catastrophe which appeared to be coming. In 1905 she received the Nobel Prize for Peace in acknowledgment of her dedicated efforts toward peace. She died on 21 June 1914, two months before the eruption of the first world war.[112]

The Age of the Female II: Heroines of the Shift

Selma Ottilia Lovisa Lagerlof
Nobel Prize - Literature

1909

In appreciation of the lofty idealism, vivid imagination
and spiritual perception that characterize her writings.

Born in Mårbacka in the province of Värmland in southern Sweden, Selma Lagerlöf became the first female writer to ever win the Nobel Prize for Literature (1909), writing in a romantic and imaginative manner about the peasant life and landscape of Northern Sweden.

The daughter of a retired army officer, Lagerlof was tutored at home and, in the care of her paternal grandmother, raised on fairy tales, legends, cavaliers, superstitions and the glorious past of the Värmland region of Sweden. Educationally, she studied at the Royal Women's Superior Training Academy in Stockholm and graduated in 1882 as a teacher.

Lagerlöf's first novel was entitled <u>Gosta Berlings Saga </u>(The Story of Gösta Berling) and did not do well in the marketplace in 1891 but experienced a revival in 1893 as a result of a positive review by Georg Brandes. She continued to write, and having received a fellowship from King Oscar, was able to devote herself entirely to writing. Her best selling work and most popular children's book was <u>The Wonderful Adventures of Nils</u> (Nils Holgerssons Underbara Resa Genom Sverige - 1906-1907), the story of a fourteen year old boy transformed to elf-size and experiencing wonderful adventures throughout Sweden from ground level as well as sky level, flying on the back of the farm's gander who joins a flock of geese flying northward. Maintaining a

King

strong moral message, the book was actually commissioned by the Primary School Board as an aid in the teaching of Swedish geography.

Lagerlof was appointed a member of the Swedish Academy in 1914. She wrote little during World War I and during the 1920s devoted much of her time and energy to women's causes. During the World War II era, she helped German intellectuals and artists escape Nazi persecution. Selfless by nature, she even donated her Nobel Prize medal during Finland's Winter War with the Soviets in order to raise funds for her struggling country. Lagerlof died on 16 March 1940, of a stroke.[113]

Grazia Deledda
Nobel Prize - Literature
1926
For her idealistically inspired writings which,
with plastic clarity, picture the life on her native
island and, with depth and sympathy, deal with
human problems in general.

Daughter of a prosperous landowner, Grazia Deledda was born in the Sardinian village of Nuoro, Italy. She began to write poems as early as the age of eight, and her first short stories were published in Rome and Milan in 1888 and 1889.

Her first book was <u>Sangue Sardo</u> (Sardinian Blood, 1888). Her first novel was entitled <u>Fior Di Saregna</u> (1892), followed by the book for which she became famous, <u>Anime ONeste</u> in 1895. Her work has been characterized as falling between the 19th Century literary movement of

'Verismo' and 'Decadentismo' which emphasized instincts and irrational forces.

In her life, Deledda produced some forty novels, averaging approximately one per year. Her life was somewhat restricted, however, due to the fascist regime of Benito Mussolini. In fact, her only travel abroad was in 1927 to receive her Nobel Prize. She died in Rome, Italy, on 15 August 1936.

Some of her published titles are Il Vecchio Della Montagna (The Old Man of the Mountain, 1900); Dopo Il Diverzio (After the Divorce, 1902); Elias Portolu (1903); Cenere (1904); La Madre (1920); Canne Al Vento (1913).[114]

Sigrid Undset
Nobel Prize - Literature
1928
Principally for her powerful descriptions of
Northern life during the Middle Ages.

Sigrid Undset was born in Kallundborg, Denmark. At the age of two, her family moved to Christiania, what is now Oslo, Norway. Her father died in 1893 and as the family's financial situation deteriorated, she took a secretarial job at the age of sixteen to support her mother and two sisters. She did this for ten years.

Undset's forte was writing about life in Scandinavian countries during the Middle Ages. Early novels focused on contemporary subjects, but her later works involved a modern world setting. Her first novel was Fru Marta Oulie (1907) which dealt with marital infidelity, a work which shocked some critics of the time. Her second novel, an imitation of Icelandic saga entitled Gunnar's Daughter (1909), earned her a government scholarship. She left her job and devoted herself entirely to writing. Her third novel, Jenny (1911), partly set in Rome, tells the story of a promising young artist entangled in the web of compromise between human love and artistic goals, a story sadly ending in the artist's suicide.

Undset's works in many ways mirrored her own life and the internal, religious, philosophical and psychological struggles she experienced. Her works exuded a knowledge of history with a psychological analysis and powerful style. She broke new ground with the 'domestic epic' - a sweeping drama set against a carefully studied social background, a background of realism and true life.

Some more works are: Splinten Av Troldspeilet (1917) which focused on the contradictions between new opportunities for women and their traditional values; Norske Helgner (1934) which discusses the role of religion in life; Gymnadenia (The Wild Orchid, 1929); Den Braendende Busk (The Burning Bush, 1930) and Den Trofaste Hustru (The Faithful Wife, 1936); her masterwork was the trilogy Kristin Lavransdotter (1929) which re-created a woman's life in the devout Catholic Norway of the Thirteenth and Fourteenth Centuries.

Undset fled her homeland during the Nazi occupation of the second world war and lived in the United States. She returned at the war's end and died in Lillehammer in 1949.[115]

The Age of the Female II: Heroines of the Shift

Jane Addams

Nobel Prize - Peace

1931

Sociologist

International President Women's International League

for Peace and Freedom

I do not believe that women are better than men. We have not wrecked railroads, nor corrupted legislature, nor done many unholy things that men have done; but then we must remember that we have not had the chance.

Jane Addams

Born on 6 September 1860, in Cedarville, Illinois, the eighth of nine children, Jane Addams gained global recognition in later life as a pioneer social worker, feminist and internationalist. In some ways she had an excellent head start because her father had been a state senator for sixteen years. He was also a personal friend of Abraham Lincoln.

Graduating from Rockford Female Seminary (later known as Rockford College) as the valedictorian of her class of seventeen in 1881, she went on to study medicine but terminated her studies because of poor health. She then spent twenty-one months traveling and studying in Europe, considering her future. In London's East End she and her friend, Ellen G. Starr, visited a settlement house for the underprivileged called Toynbee Hall. This became the catalyst for her life's work.

Returning to Chicago, she and Miss Starr opened their own home for the underprivileged, named Hull House after its builder. Its purpose was "to provide a center for a higher civic and social life; to institute and maintain educational and philanthropic enterprises and to investigate and improve the conditions in the industrial districts of Chicago."

Hull House was extremely successful, host to two thousand people in its second year. Classes and clubs were offered for children and adults day and night. The house grew to accommodate an art gallery, a second public kitchen, a coffee house, gymnasium, swimming pool, book bindery, circulating library, labor museum, cooperative boarding club for girls, music school and an employment bureau.

Jane Addams' reputation grew. She was appointed to Chicago's Board of Education and eventually became chairman of the School Management Committee. In 1909 she became the first woman president of the National Conference of Charities and Corrections. As a civic leader she headed investigations on sanitary conditions, narcotics, midwifery and milk supplies. Her beliefs were that women should make their voices heard in legislation and should have the right to vote.

Jane Addams pushed for peace and spoke against America's entrance into World War I and, in fact, was expelled from the Daughters of the American Revolution for her oppositional views. In 1915 she accepted the chairmanship for the Women's Peace Party, an American Organization. Addams discovered an outlet for her humanitarian energies as an assistant to Herbert Hoover in providing relief supplies of food to women and children of enemy countries, as related in her book Peace and Bread in Time of War (1922). She also served as president of the Women's International League for Peace and Freedom until 1929.

In 1926, Jane Addams suffered a heart attack from which she never recovered. On 10 December 1931, the day she was being awarded the Nobel Peace Prize in Oslo, she was admitted to a hospital in Baltimore. Her health continued to decline and she died in 1935 with funeral services being held at Hull-House.[116]

Irene Curie

Nobel Prize - Chemistry

1935

(Co-recipient, Frédéric Joliot)

In recognition of their synthesis of new radioactive elements

Not only did Madame Curie win an unprecedented two Nobel Prizes, she also gave birth to a child who would also gain fame as a Nobel laureate, her daughter, Irene, born on 12 September 1897, in Paris, France. During World War I, Irene served in the capacity of a nurse radiographer. In 1925 she became a Doctor of Science at the Faculty of Science in Paris. Her doctoral thesis focused on the alpha rays of polonium.

In 1935 Irene and her husband, Jean Frederic Joliot, were awarded the Nobel Prize for Chemistry in recognition of their synthesis of new radioactive elements, summarized in their joint paper: *Production artificielle d'éléments radioactifs. Preuve chimique de la transmutation des éléments* (1934).

In 1937 Irene Curie-Joliot became Professor in the Faculty of Science in Paris. In 1946 she accepted the position of Director of the Radium Institute. She was also a Commissioner for Atomic Energy for six years and instrumental in the construction of the first French atomic pile in 1948 and in planning a center of nuclear physics at Orsay.

Irene Curie-Joliot was deeply interested in the social and intellectual advancement of women, was a member of the Comité National de l'Union des Femmes Françaises and the World Peace Council. She was appointed Under Secretary of State for Scientific Research in 1936, was a member of several foreign academies, numerous scientific societies, an Officer of the Legion of Honour and recipient of honorary doctor's degrees from several universities.

Irene Curie died in Paris in 1956. She and her husband, Jean Frederic, had one son, Pierre, and one daughter Helene.[117]

Pearl S. Buck

Nobel Prize - Literature

1938

For her rich and truly epic descriptions of peasant life
in China and for her biographical masterpieces.

Born on 26 June 1892, in Hillsboro, West Virginia, Pearl Comfort Sydenstricker was the fourth of seven children and only one of three who survived to adulthood. At three months old her Southern Presbyterian missionary parents returned to China and Pearl spent the major portion of her first forty years there, speaking both English and Chinese.

Between 1910 and 1914 she returned to the states to attend Randolph-Macon Woman's College in Lynchburg, Virginia. Soon after graduation, and hearing of her mother's grave illness, she returned to

China. It was there she met and married John Lossing Buck in 1917. An unhappy marriage, it lasted for eighteen years. During the marriage both she and her husband taught at Nanking University. In 1927 there was a battle between elements of Chiang Kai-sheck's national troops, Communist forces and an assortment of warlords. This was known as the Nanking Incident. Several Westerners were murdered, and the Bucks escaped to Unzen, Japan, before moving back to China a year later.

Peal Buck's first novel was <u>East Wind, West Wind</u>, published by the John Day Company in 1930. In 1935 Pearl married its publisher, Richard Walsh, after she and he underwent divorces. Buck's second novel was <u>The Good Earth</u> which enjoyed tremendous success as the best selling book of both 1931 and 1932. It won the Pulitzer Prize for her, the Howell's Medal in 1935, and was adapted as a major MGM film in 1937. In 1938, less than a decade after her first book was published, Pearl S. Buck won the Nobel Prize for literature, the first American woman to do so.

In 1934 she returned to the United States to be closer to her daughter who had been institutionalized in New Jersey because of mental retardation since birth. She and Walsh adopted six more children during the following years, the family living at Green Hills Farm in Bucks County, PA, a monument now instated in the Registry of Historic Buildings.

Buck was active not only in women's rights but American civil rights. She published essays in both 'Crisis' - the journal of the NAACP, and 'Opportunity' - the magazine of the Urban League. She and her husband also founded the East and West Association, an organization dedicated to cultural exchange and understanding between

Asia and the West. In 1964 she established the Pearl S. Buck Foundation to provide sponsorship funding for children in Asian countries.

Pearl S. Buck died in 1973 and is buried at her beloved Green Hills Farm in Bucks County, Pennsylvania.[118]

Gabriela Mistral

Nobel Prize - Literature

1945

For her lyric poetry which, inspired by powerful emotions, has made her name a symbol of the idealistic aspirations of the entire Latin American world.

Born in Vicuña, Chile in 1889, Gabriela Mistral (pseudonym for her real name: Lucila Godoy y Alcayage) got a head start in the game of poetic expression, being the daughter of a dilettante poet. She taught school as an elementary and secondary teacher and began writing poetry after a lover committed suicide.

Mistral was quite active in education and played an important role in the educational systems of Mexico and Chile. During her teaching career, she taught Spanish literature, not only at the University of Puerto Rico, but also in the United States at Vassar College, Middlebury College and Columbia University. She was also involved in cultural committees of the League of Nations, was Chilean consul in Naples, Madrid and Lisbon, held honorary degrees from the Universities of Florence and Guatemala and was an honorary member of several cultural societies in Chile, Spain, Cuba and the United States.

In 1914 she published *Sonetos de la Muerte*, love poems in memory of the dead. This established her as a poet in Latin America, but her first great collection of poems, *Desolacion* (Despair) did not appear until 1922. *Temura* (Tenderness), a book of poems concentrating on childhood, was released in 1924. *Tala* was published in 1938. 1958 was the year in which her complete poetry was published.[119]

Emily Greene Balch

Nobel Prize - Peace

1946

Formerly Professor of History

and Sociology Honorary International

President Women's International League for Peace and Freedom

Emily Balch made her life transition into death after a full ninety-four years of dedication to the ideals of peace and freedom. Born in Boston on 8 January 1867, to a prosperous and prominent family, Emily Balch attended private schools in her youth and graduated from Bryn Mawr College in 1889 - the year of its first graduating class. Awarded a European Fellowship, she went on to study economics in Paris from 1890 to 1891, eventually writing *Public Assistance of the Poor in France* which was published in 1893.

As an outstanding teacher, Balch rose to the position of professor of economics and sociology at Wellesley College in 1913, impressing students with the clarity of her thought, breadth of her experience, strong-mindedness and compassion for the underprivileged. It was also

King

during these years in which she was socially active, participating in movements for increased wages and labor conditions, control of child labor, women's suffrage and racial justice.

In 1914 after the outbreak of the first world war, she realized her life work lay in helping mankind to rid the world of war. Her efforts involved her with international movements and organizations and in founding the Women's International Committee for Permanent Peace, whose named changed to the Women's International League for Peace and Freedom. She also became a member of Henry Ford's Neutral Conference for Continuous Mediation which was based in Stockholm, Sweden. In 1919, the Women's International League for Peace and Freedom (WILPF) based in Geneva, invited her to become its secretary. She accepted the offer and acted in that capacity until 1922, eventually donating her Nobel Peace Prize money to the WILPF in 1934.

Between world wars she was quite active working for peace and making herself available to governments, various commissions and international organizations, many of which were associated with the League of Nations. Her pacifistic views changed, however, as a result of Nazi excesses, and during the 1930s she sought ways and means to assist those who had been victimized by Nazi persecution.

Emily Balch's tireless work for peace continued during her entire life, even though her health was failing in her later years. She was awarded the Nobel Prize for Peace in 1946 at the age of seventy-nine. She died on 9 January 1961, at the age of ninety-four.[120]

The Age of the Female II: Heroines of the Shift

Gerty Theresa Cori

Nobel Prize - Medicine

1947

For their discovery of the course of the
catalytic conversion of glycogen [121]

(Co-recipient - husband, Carl Ferdinand)

Born on 15 August 1896, in Prague, Gerty Theresa Radnitz (Cori) became the first American woman to receive the Nobel Prize for Medicine and Physiology in 1947, sharing it with her husband, Dr. Carl Ferdinand Cori and Dr. B.A. Houssay of Argentina.

Gerty Radnitz was the oldest of three daughters. Their father was the manager of a sugar refinery, an occupation which would serve as a partial basis of his daughter's professional and scientific life. Gerty also had an uncle who was a professor of pediatrics at the University of Prague who influenced her to study medicine, which she did, graduating with a degree in medicine in 1920.

At medical school she met Carl Ferdinand Cori. They were married on 5 August 1920. Together they decided to pursue careers in medical research. Emigrating to the United States in 1922, they joined the staff of Buffalo's New York Institute of Malignant Diseases - he as an assistant pathologist, and she as an assistant biochemist. They were both naturalized as United States citizens in 1928.

The Cori's dedicated their professional lives to the study of the absorption of sugars from the intestines and the effects of insulin epinephrine on the fate of absorbed carbohydrates, glycerin formation and degradation. Thus, Gerty's early childhood background, with a father who was a manager of a sugar refinery and an uncle who was a

King

professor of pediatrics, served her well in serving humanity and, of course, in the presentation of her Nobel Prize in 1947.[122]

Maria Goeppert-Mayer

Nobel Prize - Physics

1963

For discoveries concerning nuclear shell structure.

(Co-recipient, Hans Daniel Jensen)[123]

Maria Goeppert-Mayer was the first American woman to win a Nobel Prize in Physics and only the second in the Twentieth Century. Her award was based on her theory that "the stability of atomic nuclei is due to the arrangement of the protons and neutrons in relatively fixed shells or orbits."[124] The first and only other female recipient of the Nobel Prize for Physics during the 1900s was Madam Curie in 1903, exactly sixty years earlier.

On 28 June 1906, Maria Goeppert was born in Kattowitz, Upper Silesia (then Germany). She was the only child of Maria and Friedrich Goeppert - he being a Professor of Pediatrics. Her upbringing had, therefore, a strong atmosphere of science and education, an atmosphere in which the entirety of her life would be focused, an atmosphere culminating in her major contribution to the understanding of the structure of the atomic nucleus for which she was awarded the Nobel Prize in 1963, the year of the assassination of John Fitzgerald Kennedy.[125]

Goeppert's Nobel Prize winning work began in 1948 and focused on the meaning of 'magic numbers' - those nuclei that have a special number of protons. "She postulated these numbers to be the shell numbers of a shell model, a 'nuclear counterpart to the closed shells of electrons' at the atomic level." Her association and commensurate collaboration with Johannes Hans Daniel Jensen in 1950 led to the publication of a book entitled Elementary Theory of Nuclear Shell Structure (1955). For their combined effort, they were jointly awarded the Nobel Prize in Physics for discoveries concerning the organization of neutrons and protons within atomic nuclei.

Goeppert-Mayer became a professor of physics at the University of California in San Diego, California in 1960. She also conducted research during her teaching years and encouraged women to pursue science careers. She held memberships in the National Academy of Sciences and the Philosophical Society. She died at the age of sixty-five in San Diego on 20 February 1972.[126]

Dorothy Crowfoot Hodgkin
Nobel Prize - Chemistry

1964

For her determinations by X-ray techniques of the
structures of important biochemical substances.[127]

Dorothy Crowfoot was born on 12 May 1910, in Cairo, Egypt, and stands in prestigious scientific company, being only the third woman to receive the Nobel Prize for Chemistry. She is preceded only by one name - Curie. Madam Curie won the honor in 1911, and her daughter, Irene Joliet-Curie, received the same honor in 1935. Hodgkin's contribution was not only for the determination of the structure of vitamin B-12, but also for her work which extended the bounds of chemistry. Hodgkin is known as a founder of the science of protein crystallography along with her mentor, J.D. Bernal. These two pioneers were the first to successfully apply X-ray diffraction to crystals of biological substances, beginning with pepsin in 1934.[128]

Following her reception of the Nobel Prize in 1964, Queen Elizabeth II of England acknowledged Hodgkin with the Order of Merit, the United Kingdom's highest royal order. She was only the second female bestowed with such an honor, the other being Florence Nightingale.

In 1969, Dr. Hodgkin ended a thirty-five year odyssey in her deciphering the three-dimensional structure of the protein insulin, a journey which she began in 1935. This discovery expanded the understanding of how insulin helps to lessen the symptoms of diabetes.[129]

In 1937 she married Thomas Hodgkin, son of one historian and grandson of two others. His primary field of focus was the history and politics of Africa and the Arab world.

During her life, Dr. Hodgkin was elected a Fellow of the Royal Society in 1947, a foreign member of the Royal Netherlands Academy of Sciences in 1956, and of the American Academy of Arts and Sciences (Boston) in 1958.

Dorothy Crowfoot Hodgkin died on 29 July 1994, in Shipston-on-Stour, England, at the age of eighty-four.[130]

The Age of the Female II: Heroines of the Shift

Nelly Sachs

Nobel Prize - Literature

1966

For her outstanding lyrical and dramatic writing,

which interprets Israel's destiny with touching strength.[131]

Daughter of a wealthy manufacturer, Leonie Nelly Sachs was born in Berlin on 10 December 1891. In her early life she studied music, dancing, literature and poetry. During World War II In 1940, Sachs escaped to Sweden. There she began studying the Swedish language and devoting much of her time to translating such Swedish poets as Gunnar Ekelöf, Johannes Edfelt and Karl Vennberg.

Interestingly, Sachs' poetic career didn't begin until her emigration to Sweden when she was close to fifty years old. Her works include: *In den Wohnungen des Todes* (In the Houses of Death), 1947; collections *Sternverdunkelung* (Eclipse of Stars), 1949; *Und niemand weiss weiter* (And No One Knows Where to Go), 1957; *Flucht und Verwandlung* (Flight and Metamorphosis), 1959; the miracle play *Eli* (1950); *Fahrt ins Staublose* (Journey to the Beyond), a series of her collected works in 1961.

Sachs received awards during her life from Sweden and Germany, among them the Prize of the Swedish Poets Association (1958) and the "Friedenspreis des deutschen Buchhandels" (1965).[132]

Nelly Sachs never married. After receiving the Nobel Prize in 1966, she stayed in Stockholm, continuing to live and work in a small apartment. On 12 May 1970, she died of cancer.[133]

Betty Williams & Máiread Corrigan Maguire
Nobel Prize - Peace

1976

Founders of the Northern Ireland Peace Movement

(later renamed Community of Peace People).[134]

Betty Williams was born on 22 May 1943, in Belfast, Northern Ireland.[135] Her road to being a distinguished peace advocate began when she was witness to the tragic death of three children when a car driven by an IRA (Irish Republican Army) terrorist was fired upon by British soldiers and lost control, killing the children. The aunt of the children was Mairead Corrigan with whom Williams joined forces along with Mr. Ciaran McKeown and formed the Community of Peace People organization. They began publicly demonstrating for peace in Northern Ireland. Williams and Corrigan were awarded the Nobel Peace Prize for their efforts in 1976.[136]

Traveling extensively, Williams has worked with fellow Nobel Laureates in trouble spots throughout the world to promote peace and the well-being of children in particular. She moved to the United States in 1981. Her list of honors includes the People's Peace Prize of Norway, The Schweitzer Medallion for Courage, the Martin Luther King, Jr. Award, the Eleanor Roosevelt Award and the Frank Foundation Child Care International Oliver Award, the Rotary Club International "Paul Harris Fellowship and the Peace Foundation Peace Building Award.[137] She was named by the International Platform Association as Speaker of the Year in 1984, and has served in the capacity of a visiting Professor of Political Science and History at Sam Houston State University in Huntsville, Texas. Williams also traveled to Thailand in 1993 to participate in international peace efforts. She has also been recognized as a recipient of the Carl Von Ossietsky Medal for courage from Berlin and received an Honorary Doctor of Law degree from Yale University.[138]

Betty Williams' co-recipient of the 1976 Nobel Peace Prize was, of course, Máiread Corrigan Maguire. Not only did she lose two of her nephews and one of her nieces when the car of the IRA gunman lost control, she also lost her sister, Anne, several years later, who was also severely injured in the tragedy.

Northern Ireland had become a killing ground soaked with blood in those years of internal conflict but enough was enough. Máiread, Williams and McKeown organized weekly peace marches and demonstrations to stop the violence. Unfortunately, the war raged on, but Máiread, undaunted, continued to work for peace. While the air was saturated with violence, she spoke only the language of non-violence. Her vision was for peace, not only for Northern Ireland, but for the world as well. Her voice and vision, however, fell on too many deaf ears. She was ignored, dismissed and ridiculed, but true to the image of all great peace activists, she pressed on. Says Máiread, "If we want to reap the harvest of peace and justice in the future, we will have to sow seeds of nonviolence, here and now, in the present." [139]

Rosalyn Yalow

Nobel Prize - Medicine

1977

(Co-recipients: Andrew V. Schally and Roger Guillemin)

For the development of radioimmunoassays of peptide hormones.[140]

Born on 19 July 1921, in New York City to Eastern European immigrants (Clara and Simon Sussman), Rosalyn Yalow began reading before even attending kindergarten. Her older brother, Alexander, assisted in her learning by making weekly trips to the public library to exchange books having been read for new ones to read.

In junior high school, Rosalyn's interest focused on mathematics but changed to nuclear physics when in college to such a degree that she became excited about pursuing a career in that field. In February of 1941, she received a teaching assistantship in physics at the University of Illinois. Upon arriving, she discovered she was the only female among the 400 members of the College of Engineering and was congratulated on her achievement by the Dean of the Faculty. On the first day of graduate school she met her future husband, Aaron Yalow.

Yalow received her Ph.D. in Nuclear Physics in January of 1945, during World War II and accepted a position as assistant engineer (the only female engineer) at the Federal Telecommunications Laboratory, a research laboratory of ITT. In 1946, she returned to teach physics at Hunter College. Then, through her husband and his work at Montefiore Hospital in the Bronx, she met Dr. Edith Quimby, a leading medical physicist, and began research in the medical applications of radioisotopes. Soon after, she joined the Bronx VA (Veterans Administration) as a part-time consultant and developed its radioisotope service which expanded to other VA hospitals.

In January of 1950, Yalow left her teaching position and joined the VA full time. In the Spring she met Dr. Solomon A. Berson with whom she formed a professional partnership which lasted for twenty-two years, terminated only by his death. Had he survived, he would have shared the Nobel Prize with Yalow.

The Age of the Female II: Heroines of the Shift

Their first investigations were in the application of radioisotopes in blood volume determination and later extended to studies of the distribution of globin, which had been suggested for use as a plasma expander. Such research culminated in the practical application in the measurement of plasma insulin in man and began the era of radioimmunoassay (RIA) in 1959, which is now used to measure hundreds of substances of biologic interest in laboratories worldwide.

Yalow went on to hold the title of Distinguished Service Professor at the Mount Sinai School of Medicine and became a member of the National Academy of Sciences. Honors which she achieved include: Albert Lasker Basic Medical Research Award; A. Cressy Morrison Award in Natural Sciences of the N.Y. Academy of Sciences; Scientific Achievement Award of the American Medical Association; Koch Award of the Endocrine Society; Gairdner Foundation International Award; American College of Physicians Award for distinguished contributions in science as related to medicine; Eli Lilly Award of the American Diabetes Association; First William S. Middleton Medical Research Award of the VA and five honorary doctorates.[141]

Mother Teresa
Nobel Prize - Peace

1979

Leader of the Order of the Missionaries of Charity [142]

Do not wait for leaders; do it alone, person to person.
Mother Teresa

Born Agnes Gonxha Bojaxhiu on 27 August 1910, in Skopie, Macedonia, Mother Teresa would become famous, respected, and loved worldwide for her relentless and tireless work with the poor and downtrodden, dedication for which she received the Nobel Peace Prize in 1979.

While attending a Roman Catholic elementary school at the age of twelve, Mother Teresa realized her life's mission was to help the poor, and she decided to prepare herself for missionary work. At age eighteen she left her home in Skopje and joined the Sisters of Loreto, an Irish community of nuns with a mission in Calcutta, India. After training in Dublin, she was sent to India where she took her vows as a nun, as well as her name Teresa, in 1928.

From 1929 to 1948, Mother Teresa taught at St. Mary's High School in Calcutta, but her compassion for the suffering and poverty outside the convent walls moved her to request, and subsequently receive, permission by the Catholic Church to leave her convent and work among the city's poor, becoming an official Indian citizen in that same year.[143]

In 1950 she founded a religious order in Calcutta (the Missionaries of Charity) to provide food for the needy and operate hospitals, schools, youth centers, orphanages and shelters for lepers and the dying poor. Her charity expanded throughout India and the world.

In 1971 she was awarded the Pope John XXIII Peace Prize, followed in 1972 by India's Jawaharlal Nehru Award for International Understanding and, of course, the Nobel Prize for Peace in 1979.[144] She also received the Balzan Prize for promoting peace and brotherhood among nations. Mother Teresa died on 5 September 1997.[145]

The Age of the Female II: Heroines of the Shift

Alva Myrdal

Nobel Prize - Peace

1982

Former Cabinet Minister - Diplomat - Writer.

Born in Uppsala in 1902, Alva Myrdal became a major voice in the social welfare, peace and nuclear disarmament movements of the Twentieth Century. Working closely with her husband, she was actively involved in social welfare concerns in the 1930s. Together they authored the book The Population Problem in Crisis.

In 1943, Alva Myrdal's energies and talents were involved with the Swedish Social Democratic Party with the task of drafting a post World War II program. During that same year she was also appointed to the Government Commission on International Post-War Aid and Reconstruction. In the post war years she devoted her energies to international concerns, heading the United Nations Organization (UNO) section dealing with welfare policy and being chairman of UNESCO's (United Nations Educational, Scientific and Cultural Organization) social science division.

In 1955 she was appointed Swedish ambassador to India, and in 1962 she became a member of Parliament and also served as Sweden's representative to the Geneva Conference on Disarmament in which she played an extremely active role. In 1967 she was promoted to Cabinet member and given the task of promoting disarmament. Her book, The Game of Disarmament, expresses her disenchantment at the reluctance of the then two world superpowers - the United States and the Soviet Union - to disarm their nuclear weapons.[146]

King

Personal profound commitment and keen professional insight were characteristics serving Alva Myrdal well during her life's work of fighting for peace - personal traits which also found an outlet through her active participation in the establishment of the Stockholm International Peace Research Institute, a organization dedicated to conducting "research on questions of conflict and cooperation of importance for international peace and security with the aim of contributing to an understanding of the conditions for peaceful solutions of international conflicts and for a stable peace."[147]

Barbara McClintock
Nobel Prize - Medicine

1983

For her discovery of mobile genetic elements.[148]

Born in 1902 in Brooklyn, New York, and dying in 1992, Barbara McClintock was certainly one of the Twentieth Century's most important geneticists. While seeking to explain the coloring patterns of maize (corn) seeds, she discovered mobile, transposable genetic elements.[149] She showed that genes could "transpose within chromosomes; that they could move around (the so-called 'jumping genes')."[150]

Although respected and appreciated by her peers and contemporaries, McClintock's work was not immediately recognized or acknowledged, and, in fact, had been ignored when it first appeared, simply too advanced for many to understand or comprehend at the time.[151] It would take approximately forty years for her work to receive the recognition it deserved. Yet, she was an extremely dedicated professional who possessed a pronounced capacity to solve intricate, multidimensional problems. Often misunderstood, she was one of the great thinkers of her age.[152]

McClintock earned her B.A. and Ph.D. from Cornell University, and received her Nobel Prize in Physiology and Medicine in 1983.[153] Her Nobel lecture was entitled, "The Significance of Responses of the Genome to Challenge." In concluding her lecture, she stated: *The examples chosen illustrate the importance of stress in instigating genome modification by mobilizing available cell mechanisms that can restructure genomes, and in quite different ways. A few illustrations from nature are included because they support the conclusion that stress, and the genome's reaction to it, may underlie many species formations.*

A collection of student's and colleague's essays entitled, <u>The Dynamic Genome: Barbara McClintock's Ideas in the Century of Genetics</u>, appeared in 1992, published by Plainview: Cold Spring Harbor Laboratory Press.[154]

Rita Levi-Montalcini
Nobel Prize - Medicine
1986
(Co-recipient: Stanley Cohen)
For their discoveries of growth factors.[155]

Rita Levi-Montalcini was born as one part of a female twin duo on 22 April 1909 in Turin, Italy. Her twin sister was Paola; mother, Adele

King

Montalcini, a talented painter; her father, an electrical engineer named Adamo Levi. She also had a brother, Gino, who became a well known Italian architect and professor at the University of Turin.

Infected by her sister's admiration with the writings of Swedish Nobel Laureate <u>Selma Lagerlöf</u>, Rita entertained thoughts of becoming a writer herself, but destiny demanded she play a different role in life. Contesting her father's Victorian philosophy of believing a professional career would interfere with his daughter's traditional role as a wife and mother, she nonetheless found her way into the academic life and eventually entered medical school in Turin, graduating Summa Cum Laude in medicine and surgery. This would, of course, be a professional life course of action that would eventually bring her the prestigious Nobel Prize. In fact, two of her university colleagues and friends, Salvador Luria and Renato Dulbecco, would receive Nobel Prizes before her. Distinguished genius, it would seem, runs in small circles.

Because of World War II and all of the embattled changes and political pressures within her homeland, her family (and her medical research work) kept moving from place to place for security. During one part of her ever transitory state of affairs during those years, she was hired as a medical doctor at the Anglo-American Headquarters in Florence to care for war refugees filtering down from the North. When the war in Italy ended in 1945, she and her family returned to Turin where she resumed her life in academia, as well as her neurological research involving chick embryos.[156]

After the war, she accepted an invitation to work at Washington University in St. Louis, Missouri, and by the early 1950s discovered chemicals in mice and chick embryos that promoted nerve cell growth.

Working together with Italian biologist, Stanley Cohen whom she met in 1953, Levi-Montalcini developed methods to treat burns and diseases such as cancer.[157]

Becoming a naturalized U.S. citizen in 1956, Levi-Montalcini was offered an Associate Professorship and then a Full Professorship in 1958, a position which she held until her retirement in 1977. Having established a research unit in Rome, she then divided her time between St. Louis and Rome, Italy. From 1969 to 1978, she also held the position of Director of the Institute of Cell Biology of the Italian National Council of Research in Rome.[158]

Rita Levi-Montalcini was elected to the prestigious U.S. National Academy of Sciences in 1968. In 1986 she was awarded the Nobel Prize for Medicine with Stanley Cohen for the discovery of the nerve growth factor (NGF) that causes nerve cells to grow.[159]

Gertrude B. Elion
Nobel Prize - Medicine
1988
(Co-recipient: George Hitchings)

For their discoveries of important principles for drug treatment [160]

Gertrude Belle Elion, daughter of immigrants from central Europe, was born in New York City on 23 January 1918. Excelling in high school, she was admitted to Hunter College, the women's section of the City College of New York and graduated, despite economic hardships, in 1937 with highest honors.

King

Having taught in the New York City secondary school system for a few years, she joined the Burroughs Wellcome Company in 1944 and began a twenty-three year professional collaboration with George Hitchings, a pharmacologist.

Working together, Elion and Hutchings discovered drugs for immunosuppression, gout; bacterial, parasitic and viral diseases. Their drug, acyclovir, a treatment for herpes, was a breakthrough in antiviral research.[161]

They also developed drugs for leukemia (6-MP), organ transplants (Imuran) and AIDS (AZT). In all, 40 patents bear the name of Gertrude Elion.

In addition to receiving the Nobel Prize in Medicine with George Hutchings in 1988, Elion received the Garvan Medal in 1968 and the National Medal of Science in 1991. In 1983 she retired to Chapel Hill, North Carolina and died on 21 February 1999.[162]

Aung San Suu Kyi

Nobel Prize - Peace

1991

Oppositional leader; human rights advocate [163]

Aung San Suu Kyi, born on 19 June 1945, in Rangoon (Burmese *Yangon*), was the daughter of General Aung San, commander of the Burma Independence Army. In 1947, when Suu Kyi was only two years old, her father was assassinated and her mother, Daw Khin Kyi, became a prominent public figure involved with social planning. In

1960 she was appointed Burma's ambassador to India and Suu Kyi accompanied her mother to New Delhi.

Her collegiate years began at Lady Shri Ram College in New Delhi. Suu Kyi then studied at Oxford University where she graduated with a B.A. in philosophy, politics and economics in 1967. In 1969 she traveled to New York for graduate work but postponed her studies to join the United Nations secretariat as Assistant Secretary, Advisory Committee on Administrative and Budgetary Questions. Suu Kyi married Michael Aris in 1972. They began a family and had two sons.[164]

26 August 1988. This was the defining moment in the socio-political life of Aung San Suu Kyi. On this date, following mass uprisings in her country where violent military suppression killed thousands of people, Suu Kyi addressed several hundred thousand people outside Shwedagon Pagoda, calling for a democratic government. This was her first public speech of this size, and thus her support for human rights and democracy, as well as her role of freedom fighter and leader in her country, began.

Her actions were not received well by authorities of the military junta. Yet, Suu Kyi continued to speak out defiantly and courageously against military suppression. Her speeches would draw thousands, igniting the flames of democracy, freedom and human rights among the Burmese people but also inflaming the ire and anger of authorities.[165]

In August of 1989, Aung San Suu Kyi was arrested by the military junta. However, prior to her incarceration, she delivered this message:

Within a system which denies the existence of basic human rights, fear tends to be the order of the day...A

King

most insidious form of fear is that which masquerades as common sense or even wisdom, condemning as foolish, reckless, insignificant, or futile the small, daily acts of courage which help to preserve man's self-respect and inherent human dignity.

For her selfless courage in her struggle for peace within her homeland, Suu Kyi was awarded the Nobel Prize for Peace in December of 1991. Unfortunately, because of her detention, she could not attend the ceremony in Oslo, Norway. Her sons, Alexander and Kim, accepted the coveted prize for her.

In 1995 Aung San Suu Kyi was released from house detention after six years, but she was denied total freedom to come and go in and out of the country as she wished. Her messages of freedom for her country to a global community have only been heard by telephone and video cassette. Unfortunately, the repressive policies and violation of human rights by the ruling military junta have continued unabated.[166]

Aung San Suu Kyi could have freed herself from her personal imprisonment by accepting a deal from ruling authorities that she leave Burma and withdraw from politics. Self interest, however, did not dictate her desires. Her desires were to see a free Burma, even if it meant her own enslavement and separation from her family who lived abroad and who were denied access to seeing her. Leadership has its sacrifice; sacrifice begets greatness, and such greatness is embodied in the person Burma's Aung San Suu Kyi.

The Age of the Female II: Heroines of the Shift

Nadine Gordimer

Nobel Prize - Literature

1991

Who, through her magnificent epic writing,

has - in the words of Alfred Nobel -

been of very great benefit to humanity.

Nadine Gordimer was born in Springs, South Africa, on 20 November 1923. She was the daughter of Isidore and Nan Gordimer. A geographically stationary destiny, she has lived her whole life in her homeland.

Gordimer's writing has been quite prolific, encompassing no less than 10 novels and 10 short story collections, as well as some non-fiction works. Some of her novel titles are: A Guest of Honour, The Conservationist, Burger's Daughter, July's People, A Sport of Nature, My Son's Story and None to Accompany Me. Her short story collections include Jump, Why Haven't You Written: Selected Stories 1950-1972. Non-fiction works include The Essential Gesture, On the Mines and The Black Interpreters.

As extensive as her books titles are her honorary degrees. In the United States, the Universities of Yale, Columbia, Harvard and the New School for Social Research have extolled her talents, as have Cambridge University and the University of York in England and the Universities of Cape Town and Witwatersrand in South Africa.[167]

Like Aung San Suu Kyi of Burma, Nadine Gordimer loves her country and holds a vision of an apartheid free South Africa. She began writing early in life, drawing from the pathologies and everyday realities of a radically divided South African society. More than any other writer, her works have been extolled for giving moral shape to the history of her country. Her views and ideological focus, placed poignantly on the written page, earned her the coveted Nobel Prize for Literature in 1991.

Interestingly, three of her own books were banned in her country. Yet, Gordimer continues to reside in South Africa. In spite of the political polarization and the restriction of her own published thought, she, like Nobel Peace Laureate Aung San Suu Ski, remains true to the land of her birth and its potential for political equality and social freedom.[168]

Rigoberta Menchu Tum

Nobel Prize - Peace

1992

Campaigner for human rights, especially for
indigenous peoples. [169]

Rigoberta Menchu Tum was born on 9 January 1959, and lived the life that only such a birthdate could manifest. Numerologically, 9 January 1959, translates to a 7 Lifepath (9 + 1 [January] + 1 + 9 + 5 + 9 = 34 > 3 + 4 = 7), a life script of spiritual testing, patience, understanding, and a lifepath which, if performed nobly, brings nobility and honor (see The King's Book of Numerology, Volume 1: Foundations & Fundamentals). Unfortunately, such a destiny often brings heartache, heartbreak, pain, suffering and sorrow in the process - pressures forcing the consciousness to turn inward and gain solace, but also gain substance and depth. Diamonds cannot be made without heat, pressure and time. So it is with diamonds of the human variety. The 7 Lifepath is the diamond maker.

The Indian family of Rigoberta Menchu was poor, belonging to the Quiche branch of the Mayan culture. As a teenager, Menchu became active in social reform and the women's rights movement, activity arousing considerable opposition in influential circles. Her family was accused of taking part in guerrilla activities, and eventually her father, mother and brother were arrested, tortured and killed - not uncommon atrocities committed by the Guatemalan army.

After such tragedies, Rigoberta became increasingly active in the CUC (Committee of the Peasant Union), an organization which her father founded and which she joined in 1979 at the age of twenty, one year before her father was murdered. She worked valiantly for social change and better conditions for farm workers on the Pacific Coast, her contribution often taking the form of educating the peasant population in resistance to massive military oppression.

At age 22 in 1981, she was forced into hiding and eventually fled into Mexico where she continued her fight abroad against the military oppression in her homeland. Her plight drew international attention when, in 1984, author Elisabeth Burgos-Debray wrote a book entitled, I, Rigoberta Menchú, a gripping documentary of Tum's human struggle and opposition against the tyranny of the Guatemalan army. It was translated into twelve languages and received several international awards.

The name 'Rigoberta Menchú,' like other freedom fighters before her and others who will come after her, is synonymous with courage, compassion, suffering, sacrifice and leadership. She has become internationally known as an advocate of Indian rights and ethno-cultural reconciliation in Guatemala and the Western Hemisphere.[170]

Toni Morrison

Nobel Prize - Literature

1993

Who, in novels characterized by visionary force and poetic import, gives life to an essential aspect of American reality. [171]

Born in 1931 as Chloe Anthony Wolford, Toni Morrison, the second of four children in an African-American working class family, would become a writer of immense dimension, a gifted storyteller whose work would not only be original but which would also garner a volume of critical applause and popular acclaim, unparalleled in modern letters. Also unparalleled is that Toni Morrison was the first African-American to ever win a Nobel Prize.[172]

Morrison's work has been acknowledged for its "epic power, unerring ear for dialogue and her poetically-charged and richly-expressive depictions of Black America."[173]

Morrison's book titles include: The Bluest Eye, Song of Solomon, Sula, Tar Baby, Beloved and Jazz. These works have garnered nearly every major literary award. In 1977 Song of Solomon won her the National Book Critics Circle Award; 1987 saw her receive the Pulitzer Prize for Beloved. The body of her work was rewarded with the Nobel Prize for Literature in 1993. She has also received the National Book Foundation Medal for Distinguished Contribution to American Letters in 1996, the Pearl Buck Award in 1994, the title of Commander of the Order of Arts and Letters also in 1994 from Paris and the Distinguished Writer Award from the American Academy of Arts and Letters in 1978.

Morrison's teaching posts have been no less noteworthy. Princeton University, Yale University, Rutgers University and Bard College were all graced with her literary and professorial presence. She has also received honorary degrees from the University of Pennsylvania, Sarah Lawrence College, Harvard, Dartmouth, Yale, Georgetown, Columbia and Brown Universities.

When Toni Morrison received her Nobel Prize in 1993 she stated:

> *I am outrageously happy. I heard the news early this morning from a colleague here at Princeton, and I am of course profoundly honored. But what is most wonderful for me, personally, is to know that the Prize at last has been awarded to an African-American. Winning as an American is very special-but winning as a Black American is a knockout. Most important, my mother is alive to share this delight with me.* [174]

Christiane Nusslein-Volhard

Nobel Prize - Medicine

1995

(Co-recipients: Eric F. Wieschaus and Edward B. Lewis)

For discoveries concerning the genetic control of early embryonic development. [175]

King

Christiane Nusslein was born in Germany during the fires of World War II on 20 October 1942, the second of five children. Her father was an architect; her grandfather, a professor of medicine; her mother, a painter who had given up her career for her children.

At an early age, Christiane demonstrated a keen interest in things and ideas. She read a great deal, as seems to be common with Nobel Laureates. By the age of twelve, she knew she wanted to be a biologist. Admittedly, however, she was a lazy student and seldom did her homework. If fact, she offers the following statements from teachers during her high school career:

> *Despite the fact that her talents are rather equally spread among many areas of knowledge, her performances are rather different depending on the distribution of her interests. Thus, with her strong display of self will she can be decidedly lazy in some topics over years, while in her areas of interests she performs to a degree far extending that required for normal school purposes. Thereby she gets into increasing difficulties and a certain nervosity, because she simply cannot cope with everything she would and should like to perform, and then loses stamina.* On the other hand, the statement also acknowledges that *she is gifted above average, has a critical and qualified judgment, and the talent for independent scientific work.*[176]

The trend continued in her college days, graduating in 1969 with a Diploma in biochemistry, but, as she says, *as usual for me, with rather*

The Age of the Female II: Heroines of the Shift

mediocre grades because I had not always paid attention and often had lost interest .[177]

Although obviously self-effacing and even saying she was bored with her projects, by the end of her doctoral thesis in 1973, Nusslein was not a mediocre student of biology, as her Nobel Prize would later testify. With a keen interest in molecular genetics and developmental biology, she pressed onward to post-doctoral research and began working with flies, which she loved because they fascinated her. It was her work with the genetic composition of 40,000 fruit fly families that served as the basis for her Nobel Prize, awarded in 1995.[178]

Wislawa Szymborska
Nobel Prize - Literature

1996

For poetry that, with ironic precision, allows
the historical and biological context to come
to light in fragments of human reality.[179]

According to CNN, the Nobel Prize for Literature given to Polish poetess, Wislawa Szymorska, in 1996, was the richest prize in the prestigious award's history: $1.1 million dollars. Also in the same article, Tadeusz Nyczek, a writer and literary critic, commented that Szymborska was "Poland's best female poet since the war"(World War II).[180]

To highlight Szymborska's art, and in some ways to justify their decision in a competition which could have seen others winners, the Nobel Prize academy, which keeps its deliberations secret, quoted the last stanza from her 1980 poem, "Nothing Twice," which translated into English reads: *With smiles and kisses, we prefer to seek accord beneath our star, although we're different (we concur) just as two drops of water are.* [181]

Tortures
Wislawa Szymborska

Nothing has changed.

The body is susceptible to pain,

it must eat and breathe air and sleep,

it has thin skin and blood right underneath,

an adequate stock of teeth and nails,

its bones are breakable, its joints are stretchable.

In tortures all this is taken into account.

Nothing has changed.

The body shudders as it shuddered

before the founding of Rome and after,

in the twentieth century before and after Christ.

Tortures are as they were, it's just the earth that's grown smaller,

and whatever happens seems right on the other side of the wall.

Nothing has changed. It's just that there are more people,

besides the old offenses new ones have appeared,

real, imaginary, temporary, and none,

but the howl with which the body responds to them,

was, is and ever will be a howl of innocence

according to the time-honored scale and tonality.

Nothing has changed.

The Age of the Female II: Heroines of the Shift

Maybe just the manners, ceremonies, dances.

Yet the movement of the hands

in protecting the head is the same.

The body writhes, jerks and tries to pull away,

its legs give out, it falls, the knees fly up,

it turns blue, swells, salivates and bleeds.

Nothing has changed.

Except for the course of boundaries,

the line of forests, coasts, deserts and glaciers.

Amid these landscapes traipses the soul,

disappears, comes back, draws nearer, moves away,

alien to itself, elusive, at times certain,

at others uncertain of its own existence,

while the body is and is and is

and has no place of its own.[182]

Jody Williams

Nobel Prize - Peace

1997

(Co-recipient: International Campaign to Ban Landmines)

For the banning and clearing of anti-personnel mines.[183]

Landmines. Williams. The two words are nearly synonymous. One can't say one without thinking of the other. The first is destructive; the second, the voice of destruction for the first.

Jody Williams is the founding coordinator of the International Campaign to Ban Landmines (ICBL). It was launched in 1992 by six

King

non-governmental organizations (NGOs) and expanded to more than thirteen hundred NGOs in eighty-five countries worldwide.[184] She has written, toured and spoken extensively against their use and proliferation.

Williams, a former ESL (English as a Second Language) teacher with not only a Master's Degree in Spanish (School for International Training, Brattleboro, Vermont, 1976) but a Masters Degree in International Relations from the Johns Hopkins School of Advanced International Studies (1984), has been a stalwart opponent of landmines and proponent to have them banned. Her humanitarian efforts have moved her voice into the chambers of the United Nations, the European Parliament and the Organization of African Unity.[185]

Williams' background and experience enabled her to become the driving force of the ICBL. From 1986 to 1992, she was deputy director of Medical Aid for El Salvador. Prior to that, from 1984 to 1986, she was co-coordinator of the Nicaragua-Honduras Education Project. Her Masters Degree in International Relations was, obviously, a boon.[186]

Honors bestowed on Jody Williams, as so many Nobel Laureates, are extensive. Other than her Nobel Prize for Peace awarded in 1997, her accolades include: the Distinguished Peace Leadership Award given by the Nuclear Age Peace Foundation in 1998; the Fiat Lux Award from Clark University; the Peacemaker of 1999 Award from the Oldender Foundation at the Kennedy Center; she was a Woman of the Year by Ms. Magazine (1997), as well as being one of Glamour Magazine's top ten women in the same year; she was included in Vanity Fair's Hall of Fame in 1998, as well as being included in its Most Influential Women in America series. She has received honorary doctorates from Williams College, the University of Vermont, Marlboro College and Briar Cliff College in Iowa.[187]

The Age of the Female II: Heroines of the Shift

CHAPTER THREE

ATHLETIC YIN

Body and mind in Yang and Yin
comprise each life in this dimension.
All human brain devoid of brawn
belies the truth of dusk and dawn.
Yin needs muscle, just as mind,
to balance out her womankind.
Therefore, fair maiden, seek ye sport
and give to Nobel Yin retort.

B odies are just as much a part of this creation as brains. Our minds don't exist in a formaldehyde bottle. They exist in a body, replete with bone and blood, sinew and tissue. To focus on either the body or mind to the exclusion of the other is to deny the reality of life in this creation and undermine the quality of that life. Wisdom dictates, therefore, a balance be established between brain and brawn.

The 2 energy is as much about 'others' as it is about 'her.' The realm of 'others' includes involvement, participation and competition. Therefore, within the Twentieth Century, it is natural that there existed an increase in competitive athletics for males as well as females, and because we are now in the 2nd Millennium, the activity of competitive athletics and competition in general will wax, not wane.

King

There are many advantages to competition, and although the cry exists in some circles, and perhaps rightly so, that competition breeds conflict and contention and is, therefore, not harmony-engendering, the reality is that we live in a dual dimension where the interaction of opposing forces is a natural and integral part of the play. Esoterically, such duality may not exist in higher spiritual realms which lie beyond this realm of duality, but the fact remains that on this earth, opposition is the norm, and it's not going to go away. The goal to harmony here is to create balance between opposing forces; not ignore or deny them. The forces exist. Managing them wisely is the key. Friendly competition is one means of managing and balancing these forces. It also offers a fun, meaningful and productive outlet for people to express their natural need to be competitive, oppositional and confrontational without being destructive.

The edified view of athletic competition is that we compete to test our skill, not expand our ego. Unfortunately, sometimes egos get out of control, but that does not diminish the highest and best good of the competitive format. It may, however, diminish the individual competitor or a team that loses control, but that's what competition is all about - the interplay of opposing forces and how to deal with them. How well a competitor manages those forces is the true test of an athlete. Those who do the best job of management and integration succeed, creating patterns and archetypes for the rest of us to follow, emulate and utilize to increase our skill and performance level and, hopefully, our character.

Diamonds are made under extreme heat and pressure over an extended period of time, not by a mere and casual blowing of an intermittent wind. If we want to be diamonds of the human variety, we must subject ourselves to heat and pressure over time. There is no other way. Chunks of coal left unattended, remain chunks of coal until they disintegrate into worthless black dust. Not much value in that. As human beings, if we want to avoid being chunks of coal, our spirits must be tried in fire and pressure over time to coalesce into the radiant, glowing, effulgent gem that is a diamond. Otherwise, we'll just be common ole' chunks of coal or dust. Athletic competition is one way of acquiring the heat, pressure and time to allow for the metamorphosis creating the brilliance and value of that which can be called a diamond, the most precious of gems.

Desire, dedication, determination, devotion, discipline, courage, commitment, concentration, confidence, continuity, camaraderie, conditioning, balance, humility, flexibility, focus, strength, poise, appreciation, grace under pressure (thank you, Ernest Hemingway, 1954 Nobel Laureate, Literature) - in body, mind and spirit - are all positive attributes derivable from the fires of competitive athletics. They constitute the spark and sparkle of the diamond.

That women have not been athletically competitive in the past thousand years is no mystery. The last millennium was the Age of the Male, and its inherent energies were naturally aligned with masculine energies. However, cosmic energies have now aligned with the female. It is her time to shine in many ways. Athletic competition is one of those ways, and she truly began her ascent in the Twentieth Century.

Furthermore, females have always been competitive. Ask any woman. They simply may not have been involved with the type of aggressive, physical competition that many males enjoy, have enjoyed, and find stimulating. However, the tide has obviously changed and competitive women's athletics are here to stay.

King

Major Female Athletes of the Twentieth Century

It is impossible to list every woman who has made a contribution to female athletics during the 1900s. There is a plethora of worthy candidates which deserve recognition and applause, but because of the limitations of this chapter, not all could be mentioned. Following is a sampling of a few of the major female players of the Twentieth Century who had an impact on the world athletic stage. Apologies are humbly given to those many gallant, courageous, skilled, dedicated and noteworthy women who are not mentioned here, but such a lack of inclusion in no way diminishes their contribution to the rise of the female in fields of athletic endeavor during the Twentieth Century.

Babe Didrikson Zaharias

1914 to 1956

Sports: Basketball, Baseball, Track and Field, Golf

The formula for success is simple:
practice and concentration,
then more practice and more concentration.

Babe Didrikson

Arguably the greatest female athlete of all time, Babe Didrikson Zaharias was not only an enigma, anomaly and pioneer of female athletics, she was an outright phenom. Born in Port Arthur, Texas, as Mildred Ella Didriksen on 26 June 1914, Babe changed the spelling of her surname, Didriksen, to Didrikson to emphasize her Norwegian, not Swedish, decent.

The Age of the Female II: Heroines of the Shift

There have been few men or woman as athletically gifted, diverse and successful as Babe Didrikson. In her day she was in a class of her own, even in her youth. Less than a stellar student, equipped with somewhat of a belligerent personality, not exactly popular with her classmates but donning an intense, competitive spirit with a cloak of supreme self-confidence, Didrikson was an outstanding athlete in many sports in her high school days. Basketball (her best sport), baseball, tennis, swimming and volleyball - were all within the realm of her remarkable athleticism. Between 1930 and 1932, Didrikson played for the Golden Cyclone basketball team in Dallas. As a three time AAU All-American, she led her team to a national championship in 1931, often scoring thirty or more points when a team score of twenty was respectable.

Such an achievement is noteworthy, but Babe's influence did not contain itself to basketball. When she was in Dallas, she also competed in softball and batted a walloping .400 - as a pitcher no less! How often does any baseball player ever hit .400, let alone a pitcher? [188]

What is more remarkable are Didrikson's track and field endeavors. During an AAU (Amateur Athletic Union) track meet in Evanston, Illinois, on 16 July 1932, Babe shocked the nation when, as the sole member of the Golden Cyclone Track and Field team, she scored thirty points and won the national championship - as a team of one! Coming in second place was the Illinois Women's Athletic Club with twenty-two points and twenty members! Unbelievable! Babe Didrikson's efforts were Herculean. She won six gold medals and broke four world records (javelin, high jump, baseball throw and 80 meter hurdles) in three hours on a single afternoon[189], a feat never accomplished - before or since - in the annals of track and field history.[190]

Following this stupendous showing at the AAU Championships, three weeks later Babe competed in the world's most prestigious athletic event, the Olympic Games, held in Los Angeles, California, and cemented her place in athletic history. Boldly and brashly she announced, "I am out to beat everybody in sight."[191] And she almost did, too. She won two gold medals and a silver, setting two world records in the process - one for the javelin (143 feet 4 inches) and another for the 80 meter hurdles (11.7 seconds).[192] She nearly won a third gold medal in the high jump but, after tying teammate Jean Shiley for the gold, she had her jumping style ruled illegal and was awarded the silver medal.[193]

Babe returned to Dallas to a Hero's welcome. At the end of 1932, the Associated Press voted her Woman Athlete of the Year, an award which she would go on to win an additional five times: 1945, 1946, 1947, 1950, and 1954.[194]

After the 1932 Olympic Games, Babe turned her athletic abilities to golf. On 23 December 1938, she married professional wrestler, George Zaharias, who became her manager, and in 1940 she won the Texas and Western Open golf tournaments. Her golfing exploits were stellar. Aside from co-founding the LPGA (Ladies Professional Golf Association),[195] during the 1946-1947 seasons, Babe Didrikson Zaharias won 17 straight tournaments, including the British Women's Amateur - the first American to do so. Again, another athletic accomplishment unparalleled and unmatched in the history of a sport. This time, of course, the sport was golf.

After a bout with cancer in 1953, Babe recovered, and in only fourteen weeks after her surgery in April resumed her playing. She won five tournaments, including the United States Women's Open, and garnered her sixth Woman Athlete of the Year Award. Unfortunately, her cancer returned and she died two years later on 27 September 1956 at the age of 42.[196]

An Associated Press poll in 1950 voted Babe Didrikson Zaharias as the Outstanding Woman Athlete of the first half of the Twentieth Century.[197] However, with her list of diverse and prodigious athletic accomplishments in multiple sports - at a time when women were not that active in athletics compared to men; when women doing what she did were often frowned upon and had little external support; after demolishing world records and establishing ones that may never be equaled, let alone surpassed, and being voted an unprecedented six times as Woman Athlete of the Year by the Associated Press, as well as being Woman Athlete of the first half of the Twentieth Century, one would have to consider her as the greatest female athlete, not just of the entire Twentieth Century, but of all time. Even today, no other woman has come close to rivaling her success and diversity, except, perhaps, for Jackie Joyner Kersee. With multiple world records in multiple sports, at a time when support for her accomplishments was practically nonexistent and in which she had to go it alone with only her own courage, vision, skill and will to nourish her, the redoubtable Babe Didrikson Zaharias stands alone, arguably and irrefutably, as, perhaps, the greatest all around female athlete of all time.

Sonja Henie

Sport:: Figure Skating

1914 to 1969

She changed the face of skating.

There will never be anyone like her.

Frank Carroll

Legacy: ten consecutive world championships, three Olympic gold medals - an achievement almost certain to never be equaled in the annals of ice skating history ever again.

Think of it. How demoralizing would it be for an ice-skating competitor between 1927 and 1936, to have to compete against a person who never lost a championship during that period, who also won three consecutive Olympic gold medals (1928, 1932, 1936) and who was obviously destined for ice-skating history and greatness?[198]

Sonja Henie was born on 8 April 1912, in Oslo, Norway. As a youth, she was ranked as Norway's third best tennis player, but her fame would be made on the edges of silver blades, not off the strings of a tennis racket. Termed "Pavlova of the Ice,"[199] Henie was also "Icon of the Ice."

Sonja Henie was born into wealth, so she had many opportunities and advantages to support her talents. Private skating rinks, skating teachers and ballet lessons were afforded to her. Yet, although manifesting a picture of sweetness and modesty on the ice with her dimples, blonde hair and soft smile, she was a cutthroat competitor. Although she finished last in her first major international competition - the 1924 Olympics in Chamonix, France, at age eleven - such failure would never repeat itself. Just three years later she began her famous ten year, undefeated skate into the ice-skating history books.

Other than making ice skating popular, Henie did two things to revolutionize her sport: 1. she choreographed her own programs (not done before) and 2. she changed her competitive attire from the traditional long skirts and black skates of the day to short-skirted costumes and white skating boots.

After her competitive skating ended, she produced a traveling ice show, "Sonja Henie Hollywood Ice Revue," which toured the United States in 1940. She also starred in approximately thirteen movies. Because of her extreme skill and business acumen, Henie became a millionaire several times over. She died of leukemia on 12 October 1969 at the age of fifty-seven.[200]

Billie Jean King

Sport: Tennis

Champions keep playing until they get it right.[201]

Billy Jean King

Born as Billie Jean Moffit on 22 November 1943, in Long Beach, California, Billie Jean King, tennis legend, arguably did more to promote professional women's tennis than any other player in the game. As a true pioneer, the female tennis players and stars of today owe her a debt of gratitude for the selfless years of dedication and devotion she showered on the Game of Kings.

Billie Jean King's artistry on the court, replete with thirty-nine Grand Slam titles, six hundred ninety-five match victories, a formidable career spanning over two decades, and a 'Battle of the Sexes' tennis match with Bobby Riggs, televised nationally in 1973, whose significance actually transcended sport and which she won in three decisive sets opening the door for respectability for women in tennis, was dynamically paralleled by what she did off the court to further the royalty of the court. Truly, Billie Jean King's legacy to the game of tennis would be more of a pioneer than a player, a leader and trailblazer who used her fame and fortune to fuel the fires, fan the flames and forge the framework for females seeking their fortunes on center stage of the court royal, a court now filled with international female millionaire celebrities.[202]

King's tennis exploits garnered her an impressive list of accolades. She was selected as "Outstanding Female Athlete of the World" in 1967; Sports Illustrated named her "Sportsperson of the Year" in 1972 - the first woman ever to be so honored - and in 1973 she was named "Female Athlete of the Year." She was the first female athlete to win over $100,000 in prize money in a single season (1971).[203] In 1990, Life magazine named her one of the "100 Most Important Americans of the 20th Century. King won a total of 39 Grand Slams in singles, doubles and mixed doubles in her career[204]; a record 20 Wimbledon titles with 6 of them in singles (1966-67-68-72-73-75); she won the U.S. Open 4 times (1967-71-72-74), the French Open in 1972 and the Australian Open in 1968. She was ranked No. 1 in the world 5 times between 1966-1972, and she was in the Top 10 players in the world a total of 17 years (beginning in 1960). She is also a member of the International Tennis Hall of Fame and the National Women's Hall of Fame.[205]

The Age of the Female II: Heroines of the Shift

A vocal supporter of Title IX (the legislation banning sex discrimination in academics or athletics in schools receiving federal aid which passed in 1972), King supported equal opportunities for females as well as males. She founded the Women's Tennis Association (WTA) in 1973, the Women's Sports Foundation in 1974, as well as World Team Tennis that same year, and Women's Sports + Fitness Magazine in 1975, the first women's sports publication.[206] Without question, the legacy of Billie Jean King, pioneer and visionary, is a lustrous light to the world of tennis and a celebrated commemoration to the Game of Kings.

Wilma Rudolph
Sports: Track & Field

My mother taught me very early to believe
I could achieve any accomplishment I wanted to.
The first was to walk without braces.[207]

Wilma Rudolph's beginning years were exactly opposite to those of Sonja Henie. Rudolph, whose destiny would lead her to overcome extreme adversity in her youth and become the first female to ever win three gold medals at the Olympic Games (Rome, 1960), was born prematurely (4.5 pounds) on 23 June 1940, into a poor but honest, hardworking and honorable family, the twentieth of twenty-two children (from two marriages; accounts vary). Her hometown, Clarksville, Tennessee, was segregated, making it difficult for Wilma to get medical care from the hospital (for whites only) for the many diseases and illnesses plaguing her during her youth: measles, mumps, scarlet fever, chicken pox and double pneumonia. The most frightening medical challenge of all, however, was polio.

Against all odds, Wilma, with the love, care and support of her family, pressed on. She overcame her physical challenges, and at age 16, qualified for the 1956 Olympics, winning a bronze medal in the 4x100 meter relay. Four years later at the 1960 Olympic Games in Rome, Italy, Wilma took center stage as the fastest woman alive, winning an unprecedented three gold medals in the 100 and 200 meter dashes and the 4x100 meter relay.[208]

Wilma Rudolph's running was something to behold: beautiful, graceful, powerful, poised and . . . fast! The crowds loved her. The world loved her. Newspapers called her "The Black Pearl" and "The Black Gazelle."[209] Those who were there to watch her history-setting, Olympic-shattering performance could only gaze in awe, their minds indelibly impressed with the memory of a lifetime - the memory of grace in speed and speed in grace, crossing a finish line in victory; not simply the finish line of a race, but the finish line of triumph over adversity, the triumph of the human will and spirit over the crippling disease of polio.

When she returned to the States, her segregated hometown of Clarksville, Tennessee, wanted to give her a homecoming parade. Rudolph rejected the offer unless the event was open to both blacks and white. The victory parade took place, the first racially integrated event in the city's history.[210]

Wilma Rudolph died of brain cancer on 12 November 1994 at the age 54, but she left an awesome legacy of accomplishment and inspiration. Bob Kersee, husband and coach of one of the greatest female Olympians ever, Jackie Joyner-Kersee, said Rudolph was the greatest influence for African-American women athletes that he knows.[211]

Wilma Rudolph's accomplishments on the track brought her the United Press Athlete of the Year and Associated Press Woman Athlete of the Year awards in 1960; the James E. Sullivan Award for Good Sportsmanship in 1961, the first woman to ever receive the award; The Babe Zaharias Award in 1962; the European Sportswriters' Sportsman of the Year Award, again the first woman recipient to be so honored; the Christopher Columbus Award for Most Outstanding International Sports Personality in 1960, also its first recipient. In 1980, Rudolph was voted into the Black Sports Hall of Fame, and in 1983, voted into the U.S. Olympic Hall of Fame. She also received the Vitalis Cup for Sports Excellence in 1983 and the Women's Sports Foundation Award in 1984.[212]

Olga Korbut
Sport: Gymnastics

The XX Olympiad of the Summer Games in Munich, Germany, in 1972 would go down in history as the most terror-struck and violent in Olympic history. It would also be recognized for its showcasing of a gymnast, Belarusian, Olga Korbut, who would later be honored by the Italian agency AHCA as the "Best Sportswoman of the 20th Century in the Gymnast category."[213]

Why was the Munich Olympiad of 1972 terror-struck? Because on 5 September, eight Palestinian terrorists belonging to a PLO (Palestine

Liberation Organization) faction called "Black September" raided the Olympic Village, killed wrestling coach Moshe Weinberg and weightlifter Joseph Romano and took nine Israeli athletes hostage. Eventually, all the hostages and most of the terrorists were killed in rescue efforts to save the Olympic competitors.[214]

In spite of the terrorist raid, the games went on. As tragic as the hostage event was, the other side of the XX Summer Olympiad coin was a fearless, joyful, giggly, gymnastic waif of eighty pounds named Olga Korbut who not only captured the hearts of Olympic fans around the world and exuded a trend-setting, flamboyant style, but who would also revolutionize the sport in the process. At 17, Korbut wasn't even supposed to compete in the Olympics. She was a replacement for an injured teammate, a replacement who would not just 'stand in' for an Olympic hopeful, but a replacement who would win three gold medals (balance beam, floor exercise and team all-around) and set the gymnastic world on fire with originality. So much for replacements.

Olga Korbut, replacement Olympian, stunned the Munich gymnastic audience with her daring athletic trademark move called "The Korbut." Standing atop the high bar of the uneven bars, she would somersault backward, regrasp the same bar, spin around the low bar at her waist and then fling herself backwards up to the high bar, catching it while looking in the opposite direction![215] Chills! Goose bumps! Spectacular artistry! It was a move onlookers craved to see again and again. ABC's Wide World of Sports honored her with "Athlete of the Year"[216] because of her revolutionary contributions to the world of gymnastics and for her worldwide heart-winning, heart-warming personality.

The Age of the Female II: Heroines of the Shift

In 1975, the United Nations honored Olga Korbut with the title "Woman of the Year." In that same year she was selected as "Athlete of the Year" by the Women's Sport Foundation.[217]

Korbut returned to the Olympics four years later in Montreal in 1976, the games in which fellow competitor Nadia Comaneci of Romania would score the first perfect 10.00 in gymnastic history. In the Montreal Olympics, Korbut won no individual gold medals but did win a gold in the team all-around.

Born on 16 May 1955, Olga Korbut, besides being the first gymnast to ever do a "Korbut" on the uneven bars, was also the first gymnast to perform a back somersault on the balance beam. She was the first gymnast ever inducted into the International Women's Sports Hall of Fame in 1982[218] and was named by Sport's Illustrated as one of the top twenty-five athletes of the Twentieth Century.[219]

Tracy Caulkins
Sport: Swimming

I know a lot of people think it's monotonous,
down the black lines over and over,
but it's not if you're enjoying what you're doing.
I love to swim and I love to train. [220]
Tracy Caulkins

Born on 11 January 1963, Tracy Caulkins was the most versatile female swimmer in U.S. history.[221] She began swimming at eight years old with the condition that she only swim the backstroke in order to keep her face from getting wet. Cute. Fact is, the face got wet, very wet, and by the age of fourteen, Caulkins was a United States champion. At fifteen she was a world champion; at seventeen, an Olympic champion. So much for keeping her face out of water.

In her stellar swimming career, Tracy Caulkins won U.S. National Titles in all four competitive swimming disciplines: freestyle, breaststroke, butterfly and backstroke. She also won the individual medley - the event consisting of all four strokes. Additionally, she set 63 American records, 5 world records and won an impressive 48 individual titles.[222]

One of the clouds of Caulkins' competitive life, as was the case of every American athlete training to participate in the 1980 Olympics, was an American-led boycott of the games which were held in Moscow. Over sixty nations refused to compete at the Olympics that year in protest of a Soviet invasion of Afghanistan in December of 1979.[223]

At the World Championships in Berlin in 1978, Caulkins won five gold medals and a silver and was hoping for Olympic gold in the 1980 Olympics. Unfortunately, the boycott obviated such dreams. Caulkins had to wait until the Los Angeles Olympics of 1984 before she could gain the gold medals which had eluded her - elusion by political decree, not personal desire. However, destiny could not deny her desire for gold, and in the LA Games Tracy won the 200 and 400 meter individual medley, as well as the women's medley relay. After the 1984 Olympics, Caulkins retired from swimming, leaving a legacy of supremacy for future swimmers to chase.[224]

A few of Tracy Caulkins' hallmarks and awards along the way: reception of the Sullivan Award in 1978 as the nation's outstanding amateur athlete, the youngest person ever to receive such an honor; the surpassing of Johnny Weismuller's (of Tarzan fame) record of 36 national titles, which she accomplished in 1981 and 1982; the acquisition of twelve NCAA championships during her collegiate career at the University of Florida from 1982 to 1984; reception of the Broderick Cup in 1982 as the nation's outstanding female college athlete; inductee into the International Women's Sports Hall of Fame, the U.S. Olympic Hall of Fame and the International Swimming Hall of Fame.[225]

Nadia Comaneci
Sport: Gymnastics

Hard work has made it easy. That is my secret.
That is why I win.[226]
Nadia Comaneci

It was a moment unheralded in gymnastic history, a moment to behold; a moment to remember . . . forever. The place: Montreal, Canada. The year: 1976. The event: the Summer Olympic Games. The moment: an unprecedented score of 10.00 by Romanian gymnast, Nadia Comaneci, after her performance in the compulsory round of the uneven parallel bars.[227]

Comaneci's score of a perfect 10.00 was the first of its kind in the Olympic gymnastic world, a world which had never seen anything like it. It was a moment of goose bumps, a moment where the hair stood up on the skin and chills ran up the spine, a moment where tears rolled down cheeks and hearts smiled with wonder. It was an awe-inspiring moment in competitive history that history had never seen and would never see again. Generated by a waif of a fourteen year old who would become the darling of the 1976 Olympics, it was a moment unparalleled in sport, and it commenced from a competitor named Comaneci in an event showcasing parallel bars that were themselves, unparalleled.

Comaneci was born on 12 November 1961 in Onesti, Romania. During the Montreal Olympic Games, with the world and her coach - the ubiquitous and indefatigably supportive Bela Karolyi looking on - Nadia not only became the first person to ever score a perfect 10.00 in Olympic competition, she was also the youngest Olympic AA champion ever at 14.[228] In the 1976 Games, she won five medals: 3 gold (uneven bars, balance beam, women's all-around), a silver in women's team, and a bronze in floor exercise. In the 1980 Olympics in Moscow, Comaneci won 2 more gold medals (balance beam and floor exercise) and 2 silvers in women's all-around and women's team, bringing her Olympic cache to 5 golds, 3 silver and 1 bronze.[229] Her last competition was in 1981 at the University Games where she won 5 gold medals:[230] one each in the vault, balance beam, uneven bars, floor exercise and the women's all-around, scoring two more 10.00s: one in vault and the other in floor X.[231]

During her stellar and renowned athletic career, Nadia Comaneci had solidified herself as the darling heroine of women gymnastics. However, finding herself in the uncomfortable position of being a symbol of success in an impoverished country, she defected Romania in 1989, moved to Norman, Oklahoma, and married Bart Conner, an American gymnastics star in 1996.[232]

The Age of the Female II: Heroines of the Shift

Julie Krone

Sport: Horse Racing

I don't want to the be the best female jockey in the world;
I want to be the best jockey. [233]

Julie Krone

There are few things more exhilarating and potentially perilous in this world than the oneness experienced by being on a horse's back at a full gallop. For both the horse and rider there is athleticism, intensity and danger, especially in a competitive event. There is also a definitive calling for courage and the near embracing of a devil-may-care attitude. It's one thing to be an athlete in the fire of competition relying solely upon your own skills, but it's entirely another thing to also have to rely on a horse and his skill to propel you to victory, especially when your life and well-being, as well as those of the horse, are at risk. If the horse stumbles and falls, the results can be disastrous for both horse and rider, and the frighteningly poignant concern is that that moment of catastrophe can happen in the blink of an eye, in a split second, at any second, and . . . such catastrophes can be horrifyingly unforgiving, their results irreparable, lamentable and tragic, as history as proven time and time again.

Such is and was the world of Julie Krone, jockey, a world dominated by masculine yang whose prejudices disapproved of females at the racetrack, a world also where the myth of women lacking the physical strength, mental toughness and aggressive mindset to compete at the zenith of the "sport of kings" was extant. It was a world needing to be challenged, a world whose myths needed shattering. And so they were.[234]

Differences of opinion create challenges. They also make horse races. Julie Krone spent her professional life racing horses. She also spent it in another race, the race of proving that women jockeys are every bit as good as men, can compete with men and . . . beat them in a game they thought, erroneously, belonged to them.

Born Julieanne Louise Krone on 24 July 1963 in Benton Harbor, Michigan,[235] Julie Krone began riding horses before she could walk, growing up on a farm near Eau Claire, Michigan, the daughter of a champion horsewoman. Prevaricating lightly about her age, Krone secured a summer job as a workout rider at Churchill Downs, home of the Kentucky Derby, when she was 15 in 1979. Subsequently, she quit high school in her senior year, made her way to the Tampa Bay Downs racetrack in Florida, got her first professional race on 30 January 1980, at the age of 16 and won the race! It was a fortuitous omen. By the time she concluded her horse racing career, Julie Krone had become the winningest and most successful female jockey of all time, garnering 3,456 victories and earning $81 million in purses during her remarkable and premier eighteen year career.

Krone had an impressive list of firsts. She was the first woman to win the leading rider title at a major track, twice in fact. The first was at Monmouth Park in New Jersey in 1987 and the second at Gulfstream Park in Florida in 1992/1993. She was also one of only four jockeys to win six races in one day. This she did on 19 August 1987, at Monmouth Park. She was also the first woman to compete in the Breeders' Cup (1988).[236]

The Age of the Female II: Heroines of the Shift

The apex of Julie's racing career came on 5 June 1993, at the Belmont Stakes, one of horse racing's coveted Triple Crown venues. The other two are the Preakness and the Kentucky Derby. Riding aboard Colonial Affair, a 13 to 1 longshot, Krone made horse racing history with her unprecedented victory, being the first woman to win the Belmont Stakes and, therefore, to ever win a Triple Crown race.[237]

Krone's career was not without its manifested perils. She shattered her left arm in a fall at the Meadowlands in 1989, suffered a severely broken ankle and a cardiac contusion in 1993 when she was kicked in the chest by her horse and fractured her left hand at Gulfstream Park in 1995. The wear and tear on her body took its toll, but before she retired, she won the last three races of her outstanding career on 25 April 1999, at Lone Star Track in Grand Prairie, Texas.[238]

As she is quoted as saying at the time of her retirement:

I'm on top, I'm 35 years old, and there are other things I want to do. Physically, there is a lot of pain. I don't want to be hurt again. I have nothing left to prove.[239]

Bonnie Blair

Sport: Speed Skating

*I'm definitely going to miss hearing
the sound of that gun.*[240]
Bonnie Blair

Speed. Wind. The sound of a starter's gun . . . and gold, lots of gold; in fact, more gold than any American female had ever seen in Olympic history, 5 medals of gold in all, and it all belonged to a woman who, since childhood, simply loved to create wind around her as she raced around a track of ice on silver blades.

Bonnie Kathleen Blair was born on 18 March 1964, in Cornwall, New York. "Blur" as she was called, won gold medals in the same event in 3 consecutive Olympic Games, becoming the winningest American in Winter Olympic history.[241]

Those events were the 500 meters at the 1988 Olympics in Calgary, Alberta, Canada and 1992 Games in Albertville, France where she also won the 1,000 meters. Then in 1994 in Lillehammer, Norway, she collected more gold in the 500 and 1,000 meter races. In all, 5 sparkling and extremely valuable Olympic gold medals, more than any other female in the history of the prestigious games.[242]

Bonnie the "Blur" Blair began her skating experience early at age four. By her own account, all she ever wanted to do was skate. She was the youngest of six children, four of whom were speed skaters. She practiced in her early years at a rickety ice rink in Champaign, Illinois. She won U.S. indoor titles in 1983, 1984 and 1986. She was the North American indoor champion in 1985. In her first Olympic Games in Canada (1988), "Blur" set a world record in the 500 meters on her way to her first gold medal. In 1989 she won the World Over-all Sprint title, and then repeated her 500 meter sprint to gold in the 1992 Albertville games. At the 1994 Norway games, Blair ended her career with gold-winning performances in the 500 and 1,000 meter races.[243]

Without question, Bonnie Blair is the best speed skater America has ever produced. The coach of the U.S. speed-skating team, Peter

Mueller (also an Olympic gold medalist), said of Blair, she's "the best technician in the world over the sprint distance (500 and 1000 meters), man or woman. It's like she was born on the ice."[244]

Bonnie Blair's list of accolades: she was the only U.S. Winter Olympian to win a gold medal in the same event in three Consecutive Olympics. World record holder, 500-meter speed skating: 38.69 seconds, set February 1995, in Calgary, Canada. The Associated Press 1994 Female Athlete of the Year. The 1994 Sportsperson of the Year by Sports Illustrated. World record-holder for overall points (156.505). World record-holder in the 500 meters (38.99 seconds), Calgary, March 1994. U.S. National Sprint Champion, 1985-94. United States Olympic Committee's Sportswoman of the Year, 1992 and 1994. USOC's (United States Olympic Committee) Woman Speedskater of the Year, 1985-94. Glamour magazine's Women of the Year Award, 1994. James E. Sullivan Award (nation's top amateur athlete), 1992.[245]

Cheryl Miller
Sport: Basketball

For a sport to emerge onto center stage, it needs a star. For women's basketball, that star came in the presence of Cheryl Miller who, says Louisiana Tech coach Leon Barmore unequivocally, "was the best player this game has ever had."[246] That's high praise, very high praise - to be the best player a game has ever had!

First of all, Miller was a four-year All-American high school standout, averaging 32.8 points and 15 rebounds per game for 90 games at Poly High School in Riverside, California. Once she even scored an unbelievable 105 points in a single game in 1982 (let's hear it, Wilt the 'Stilt' Chamberlain).

Miller's dominating influence in college elevated women's basketball to a new level. Attending USC (University of Southern California), she was a four-time All-American and a consecutive three-time Naismith Player of the Year from 1984 to 1986, an award given to the nation's outstanding female basketball player. Miller also led USC to two NCAA (National Collegiate Athletic Association) championships in 1983 and 1984, as well as anchoring the United States women's basketball team to Olympic gold in 1984 in Los Angeles to the delight of her alma mater's hometown fans. Miller also acquired gold medals in the Pan American Games in Caracas, Venezuela in 1983 and the Goodwill Games in Moscow in 1986.[247]

Graduating in 1986, and corroborating Leon Barmore's views, Sports Illustrated named Cheryl Miller the best basketball player in the nation, male or female! In celebration of her outstanding collegiate career, USC recognized her by retiring her basketball jersey, #31, making her the first Trojan athlete, male or female, to ever be so honored.[248]

Joan Benoit Samuelson
Sport: Track & Field

It's funny. I'm attracted to things that don't have any impact on life. People say I've done a great thing for women. I don't think I have. People say I've given

people courage. That makes me feel good, but I don't
see how I do that. I think my running is a selfish thing.
But it provides the challenge that allows me to feel
good about myself. How can I expect to do well in
other activities if I don't feel good about myself. [249]

You're right, Joan, you can't. We all need to feel good about ourselves, and maybe that's the key to why you've been an inspiration to others, notwithstanding your humility. It's takes courage to be yourself, and through your courage, we have a living example to develop ours. Once somebody opens the door and walks through it, it's easier for others to follow. Maybe that's why people say you've done great things, not just for women, but for everyone. You opened the marathon championship door for females, and if going through that door a second time to prove that it could be done wasn't enough, you did it again. Then to show the world it wasn't luck, you 'walked' through it a third time and crowned it all off with Olympic gold. By anybody's standards, that's remarkable and . . . inspirational. It's the stuff champions are made of, the stuff legends are made of. That's why the applause is directed your way, Joan. Thank you.

Joan Benoit Samuelson was born on 16 May 1957 in Cape Elizabeth, Maine. Inspired by her two older brothers, she took up running after she broke her leg skiing. In 1979 while attending Bowdoin College in Maine, she entered the Boston Marathon. She won. Her time: 2:35:15 - an American record.

After surgery to repair her damaged Achilles tendons in 1981, Samuelson entered the Boston Marathon again in 1983. She won again, this time setting a world record of 2:22:43. When the 1984 Olympic

Games arrived, Samuelson was not favored to win. Grete Waitz of Norway was. But to get the gold, you've got to run the race. That's what sports are all about - head to head competition. For Joan Samuelson, Olympic history would be made when the starter's gun fired. Although not favored to win, she took the lead of the inaugural women's Olympic marathon in the third mile of twenty-six miles and never looked back. Passing through the tunnel and into the stadium of the Los Angeles Coliseum to finish the race, she recounted: "When I came into the stadium and saw all the colors and everything, I told myself, 'Listen, just look straight ahead, because if you don't, you're probably going to faint.'"[250]

Joan Benoit Samuelson didn't faint, and she didn't choke. She won Olympic gold. It was a hallmark day because never before in the entire history of the Olympic games had there ever been a marathon just for women. That year, 1984, there was, and Samuelson was given the opportunity of triumph, which she accepted, and the concomitant distinction of the being the first woman in the history of the world to win an Olympic Marathon.[251]

In 1985 Samuelson ran again and won, again, setting an American record at the Chicago Marathon with a time of 2:31:21. It was in this year of 1985 that Joan Samuelson was awarded the Sullivan award as the outstanding amateur athlete in the United States.[252] Without question, the accomplishments of Joan Benoit Samuelson set a standard for others to follow, accomplishments lifting the athletic value of women in the eyes of the world, accomplishments which made her, not just a hero, but a legend.

The Age of the Female II: Heroines of the Shift

Jean Driscoll
Sport: Wheelchair Racing

Successful people are those who've fallen off the
horse a dozen times and gotten back
on a dozen times. [253]
Jean Driscoll

What Joan Benoit Samuelson did for women's foot racing, Jean Driscoll did for wheelchair racing. As Samuelson got her running start in high school, so did Driscoll, born with spina bifida, a birth defect which interferes with the development of the central nervous system: the brain, the spinal cord and the nerve tissues.[254]

Driscoll competed in her first wheelchair race, the Chicago Marathon, in October of 1989, finishing second. A year later, in 1990, Driscoll went on a rampage, winning seven straight Boston Marathons, setting and re-setting her own world records. Destiny seemed to deny her another victory, but then in 2000, she won the Boston Marathon for the eight time, a feat never before accomplished in the one hundred five years of the event.[255]

In Olympic competition, Driscoll won two silver medals, setting an American record at Barcelona in 1992. Her second silver came in Atlanta in 1996. In the Paralympic Games (held two weeks after the Olympic Games in the same host city) she won an impressive five gold medals, three silver and four bronze medals. These were won in 1988 in Seoul, Korea; 1992 in Barcelona, Spain; 1996 in Atlanta, Georgia and 2000 in Sydney, Australia.[256]

Driscoll's courage to press on and triumph in the face of adversity has made her a world renowned motivational speaker. She holds a plethora of awards, including Women's Sports Foundation Amateur Sportswoman of the Year in 1991, USA Track and Field Disabled Female Athlete of the Year in 1992, Wheelchair Sports U.S.A. Female Athlete of the Year in 1992 and 1996, the Illinois Fellowship of Christian Athletes Champion in Christ Award in 1996, the Athletes International Ministries Female Athlete of the Year in 1997, and the Gene Autry Award in 1997. *Sports Illustrated for Women* named her as one of the top 25 female athletes of the Twentieth Century.[257]

Evert/Navratilova
Sport: Tennis

Rivalry. It's the essence of sport. Without it, there would be no sport. There would also be no memories, memories manacled to the mind with the tentacles of an unrelenting octopus, never letting one escape from the thrill, the wonder, the tension, laughter, tears, triumphs and defeats of adrenaline in overdrive.

The world of sport has bequeathed to its citizens of sport a register of rivalries which have become timeless household parlance: Chamberlain/Russell, basketball; Ali/Frazier, boxing; Palmer/Nicklaus, golf; Dodgers/Giants, baseball; Fischer/Spassky, chess; India/Pakistan, cricket; Raiders/Chiefs, football; Borg/McEnroe, men's tennis and the femmes fatales of the tennis turf, Evert and Navratilova.

Chrissy Evert and Martina Navratilova gave the tennis world of the Twentieth Century fifteen years of the greatest female rivalry of all time. Each alone was a star. Of this there is no question; no doubt. Their styles and personalities were as contrasting as Yin and Yang; their ever ubiquitous exchange of being the No. 1 tennis player in the world was like a teeter-totter in fifth gear. They were magnetic, mesmerizing and marvelous to watch. What they did for women's tennis cannot be measured except in memory, unforgettable memory.

Evert, older by two years, won twenty-three of their first twenty-nine meetings. However, by the end of their careers, Navratilova owned a decisive forty-three to thirty-seven edge. Navratilova won a 167 singles titles; Evert, 157. Between the two of them, the pair won 18 out of the 19 Grand Slams between 1982 and 1986. Talk about domination. Interestingly, at competitive career end, each had won 18 Grand Slam titles.[258]

Evert/Navratilova was an epic rivalry beyond compare; their respect, mutual; their fame only amplified, not diminished, by the other. These two Hall of Fame females were so inextricably intertwined that they even ended up settling in the same community upon their retirement - Aspen, Colorado.[259] Who was the better player? Does it matter? What matters are the memories, the motivation and inspiration this dynamic competitive duo gave to the tennis world. Tennis rivalries they were in this life, to be sure. Perhaps they may even be sisters in the next. Only God knows, but one thing is certain: Chris Evert and Martina Navratilova were champions at heart, great for the game of tennis and unquestionable icons of their time.

Steffi Graf
Sport: Tennis

Tennis legend, pioneer and entrepreneur Billy Jean King had, perhaps, the most succinct and direct quote regarding German born tennis icon, Steffi Graf. Says King, "Steffi is definitely the greatest women's tennis player of all time." It doesn't get any more adulatory than that. To have one of the greatest tennis luminaries of all time invoke another as being the greatest of all time speaks volumes.

And not that Steffi Graf's career was not voluminous. Born Stephanie Maria Graf on 14 June 1969 in Mannheim, Germany,[260] Steffi was introduced to tennis at the tender young age of four by her parents, her father acting in the capacity of her primary coach through her early career. At age seventeen, four years after turning pro at age thirteen, Graf stunned the tennis world by beating tennis great Chris Evert at Hilton Head in 1986, Evert being sixteen years her senior. After dispatching Evert, Graf went on to dispatch the reigning queen of tennis, Martina Navratilova in the Berlin final and the French Open. A new Queen of the Courts had arrived, and she would become the winningest female tennis star in history.[261]

It's hard to comprehend Graf's prodigious accomplishments. For example, to be rated as the #1 athlete in any sport during any given year is, indeed, an honor warranting the highest esteem, especially because one is continually competing against the best players in the world, which simply means that if an athlete is regarded as #1 in his sport, he is duly recognized as the absolute best of the best. Steffi Graf was #1 in the world of women's tennis, but not just for a year. During her stellar career, Steffi Graf was rated as the #1 tennis player in the world for an impressively gaudy 377 weeks! That's 7 and 1/4 years of being the best of the best in the entire world. At one point, Graf remained at #1 for 186 consecutive weeks - that's 3.5 years. What professional athlete can say that he or she has ever embraced such a #1 Rated legacy? Answer: no one. No player, male or female, has ever equaled such a mark.[262]

In her jaw-dropping, eye-popping, head-shaking, unbelievable career, Graf, who compiled a total of 22 Grand Slam victories in seventeen years before retiring at age 30, is the only player to have won all four Grand Slam events at least four times (Australian-4, French Open-6, U.S. Open-5 and Wimbledon-7).[263] She also won 102 championships, including the Gold medal at the 1988 Seoul, South Korea, Olympics. Her career win/loss record was 905 wins to only 115 losses. Staggering! Simply staggering![264] It is in consideration of her enormous, nay, prodigious accomplishments, that Billie Jean King extolled Graf as being the greatest women's tennis player of all time - a very gracious and classy remark from a great woman, not just a great champion.

Steffi Graf announced her retirement on 13 August 1999. She married fellow tennis great, Andre Agassi. Their first child was a boy. How interesting it will be to follow his destiny. Will he follow in the cavernous foot steps of his parents, or will he follow another path? Time will tell, but one thing is certain: if he chooses to become a tennis player, he'll never have to hire a coach!

King

Peggy Fleming

Sport: Ice Skating

The first thing is to love your sport.
Never do it to please someone else.
It has to be yours.[265]

Peggy Fleming

She is the absolute apotheosis of Yin, the perfect example of beauty, poise, power and grace, and a face, says Phil Hersch of Sports Illustrated, "that launched a thousand zambonis."[266] Notwithstanding Hersch's comment, Helen of Troy would have been lucky to stand in the shadow of Peggy Fleming. Arguably, no other athlete in any sport has graced life with greater elegance than she.

Born Peggy Gale Fleming on 27 July 1948 in San Jose, California,[267] Peggy Fleming did more for women's ice skating than anyone in the modern era. In fact, she launched the modern era. Although other athletes have won more gold medals than she, no athlete has radiated an aura of gold quite like she. Peggy Fleming is the quintessential paradigm of a champion - exquisitely skilled in her craft, gracious and humble in her manner, magnetic and charismatic by nature.

Who could ever forget the unforgettable - a beautiful, young, athletic, artistic, graceful, elegant, nineteen year old female ice skater, dressed in gold, gliding to gold in the Tenth (X) Winter Olympiad held in Grenoble, France, in 1968.[268] It was the only gold medal the United States would win in the Olympic games that winter, but a gold medal of alchemical magic, for it was Fleming's performance that transformed a common competitive event into <u>the</u> glamour event of the Winter Olympics, setting a new standard for artistic, athletic elegance on the ice.[269]

In her career, Peggy Fleming won 5 consecutive U.S. Figure Skating Championships (1964 -1968); 3 consecutive World Figure Skating Championships (1966 - 1968) and, of course, the gold medal at the Grenoble Olympics. In that Olympic year, the Associated Press named Fleming as their Female Athlete of the Year. She has been inducted into the World Figure Skating Hall of Fame, the International Women's Sports Hall of Fame and the Olympic Hall of Fame.[270]

In 1999, Fleming was honored at the Sports Illustrated 20th Century Awards as one of the most influential athletics of the Twentieth Century. She has been invited by four different administrations to perform at the White House. She has also been a television commentator and spokesperson for many humanitarian causes and foundations, as well as helping, supporting and encouraging countless thousands of women by sharing her struggle with breast cancer.[271]

What is most noteworthy about Peggy Fleming, however, is that, not only in her professional life but in her personal life as well, she has never allowed the seductive aspect of fame to inflate her ego. She has worn her gold like a true champion, not on the outside, but on the inside, radiating outward for all the world to see and share.

Janet Guthrie

Sport: Auto Racing

You cannot afford to get angry behind the wheel.
A good driver needs emotional detachment,
concentration, good judgment, and desire. [272]

Janet Guthrie

I then bequeath the whole of my property...to the United States
of America, to found at Washington, under the name of the
Smithsonian Institution, an Establishment for the increase &
diffusion of knowledge... [273]

James Smithson (1765-1829)

The Smithsonian is committed to enlarging our shared
understanding of the mosaic that is our national identity by
providing authoritative experiences that connect us to our
history and our heritage as Americans and to promoting
innovation, research and discovery in science. These
commitments have been central to the Smithsonian since its
founding more than 155 years ago. [274]

Lawrence M. Small, Secretary of the Smithsonian

Why these two quotes regarding the Smithsonian Institution? Because they lend corroborative support to the credentials of Janet Guthrie, the first woman to ever race in the prestigious Indianapolis 500, and whose racing helmet and suit are displayed in the Smithsonian

Institution. What athlete can say their jersey, helmet or shoes are on display at the world renowned Smithsonian?

Obviously, Janet Guthrie and her accomplishments are not to be taken lightly, nor is she a typical athlete. Guthrie's background is diversified. Graduating from the University of Michigan in 1960 with a B.S. in Physics, she became a research and development aerospace engineer, involved with programs which were precursors to Project Apollo. Guthrie actually applied for the Scientist-Astronaut program and made it through the first round of screening. She was a pilot, flight instructor, technical editor and public representative for some of the country's major corporations.

Guthrie loved cars . . . and racing as well. Her career in physics gradually gave way to a career in racing on a full-time basis. Before being invited to test a car for the Indy 500, she had been building, maintaining and racing sports cars for thirteen years. In 1977[275] she competed in her first Indy 500 but engine trouble forced her out of the race. In 1978 she competed again, this time finishing 9th. In all, Guthrie participated in Indy car races eleven times and won $84,608. Her last major race was in the 1979 Milwaukee 200 where she finished fifth.[276]

As well as being the first woman to compete at the Indianapolis 500, Guthrie, was also the first woman to compete in a NASCAR Winston Cup super speedway stock car race (1976). She remains the only woman to lead a Winston Cup race(Ontario, CA, 1977) and to finish a Winston Cup race as Top Rookie. In 1977 she was the first woman and Top Rookie at the Daytona 500. Additionally, Janet Gurhrie was one of the first athletes named to the International Women's Sports Hall of Fame.[277]

King

Mia Hamm

Sport: Soccer

No-one gets an iron-clad guarantee of success.
Certainly, factors like opportunity, luck and timing
are important. But the backbone of success is usually
found in old-fashioned basic concepts like hard work,
determination, good planning and perseverance. [278]

Mia Hamm

When Mia Hamm scored her 108th international goal against Brazil in Orlando, Florida, on 16 May 1999, she became the world's all time leading scorer. As the most recognized female soccer player in the world, FIFA (Federation Internationale de Football Association) named her the Women's Player of the Year for 2001 and 2002, the first two years in which the world's governing soccer body bestowed the award on a woman. At the end of the 2002 season, Hamm became the world's all-time leading scorer with 136 goals, 114 assists for a total 386 points (all team records). She was the second most capped player in the world behind teammate Kristine Lilly ('cap' is a term used to acknowledge international game appearances). With her tremendous assist record, even if Hamm had never scored a goal, she would still be among the top ten scorers in U.S. history, a statistic that enabled her to win U.S. Soccer's Chevy Female Athlete of the Year Award five consecutive years from 1994 to 1998.[279]

Adding to her scoring honors, Hamm's striking capability helped the University of North Carolina to win four NCAA titles. She also has won an Olympic gold medal and two World Cup championships. In

1997 she was named the Women's Sports Foundation Athlete of the Year by Sports Illustrated and People Magazine named her as one of the 50 most beautiful people.[280]

Born on 17 March 1972, and growing up an as Air Force brat, Mia Hamm was the youngest woman ever to play with the U.S. National Team at the age of 15 and, at the age of 19, she was the youngest member of the 1991 women's world championship team. In 1995 she was MVP (Most Valuable Player) of the Women's World Cup in Sweden. Her first international soccer appearance was against China on 3 August 1987, and her first international goal against Norway on 25 July 1990.[281]

Mia Hamm's influence on the game of soccer cannot be underestimated. With the growth of female soccer worldwide, Hamm's driving excellence, ubiquitous presence around the net and lethal striking capability have motivated countless young women around the world to either take up soccer or improve their own soccer game, fueling the fires of growth and expansion of worldwide soccer in the years and decades to come.

In fact, Mia Hamm was part of, perhaps, the greatest female competitive event in history - the 1999 World Cup Final held at the Rose Bowl in Pasadena, California, on the 10th of July in which the United States defeated China 1-0. It was one of the most intense and electrifying moments in sports history, witnessed by the largest crowd to ever watch a women's sports event in person - 90,185 fans. After a full 90 minutes of regulation play and two sudden-death overtimes, the U.S. finally got the win when Brandi Chastain slipped a penalty kick past China's goalkeeper, Gao Hong.[282] It was a volcanic moment for the U.S., coming at the end of a spine-tingling game in which either side had opportunities to put the other away. But, unfortunately, only one team could win, as is the nature of sports. Still, that World Cup Final between two highly skilled and courageous women's soccer teams - the United States and China - was, irrefutably and undeniably, one of the greatest moments in all of sports and did more for the future of women's soccer, perhaps, than any other single event, and it came in the last year of the Twentieth Century - only micro-moments before the official onset of the Age of the Female, the 2nd Millennium.

Nancy Lopez
Sport: Golf

I love the challenge.[283]
Nancy Lopez

Roswell, New Mexico. It's name conjures up images of alien spaceships and governmental cover-ups. But Roswell has another claim to fame, a more athletic one, for it was once the home of Mexican-American golf standout, Nancy Lopez.

Nancy's father, Domingo, realized early on in the life of his youngest daughter that she had a special talent, an ability to swing a golf club. He believed in her so much that he built a sand trap in his back yard to compliment her practice. His efforts did not go unrewarded; nor did hers. Receiving her first set of golf clubs at age eight, Nancy won her first Pee-Wee tournament at age nine and the state championship at age ten. Solidifying herself as one of the best junior players in the country, Lopez won the New Mexico Women's

Amateur at age twelve, the USGA Junior Girls Championship in 1972 and 1974, the Western Junior three times and the Mexican-Amateur in 1975.

Lopez began a collegiate career at the University of Tulsa. She received an All-American status and was the university's Female Athlete of the Year in 1976. But the magnetic pull of professional golf became so strong that she left college in her sophomore year to pursue a professional career.[284]

Lopez's 1978 inaugural season was the most phenomenal tour for an LPGA Rookie. She won nine tournaments, five in a row and remains the only woman to be named Rookie of the Year and Player of the Year plus win the Vare Trophy for the lowest scoring average in a single season. Achievements just beginning, at age 30 in 1987, she became the third youngest player ever inducted into the LPGA Hall of Fame. Her exquisite game and her exquisite charisma made her the biggest draw in women's professional golf, so much so that to her legion of fans, the word 'golf' was actually spelled: N a n c y   L o p e z.[285]

In 1997 Nancy Lopez racked up her 48th tournament victory at the age of 40,[286] and although she had a remarkable career, because of her Mexican-American descent, she had been subjected to discrimination. Early on she was disallowed from membership in the Roswell Country Club, so she had to play in Albuquerque, some 200 miles away. The fact that she was so good as a player, and Hispanic, brought its share of criticism, but she remained undaunted and true to the profile of a true champion.[287]

In her remarkable career, Nancy Lopez was LPGA Rookie of the Year, Player of the Year, inductee into the LPGA Hall of Fame and a recipient of the United States Gold Association's 1998 Bob Jones Award.[288]

Margaret Court
Sport: Tennis

My femininity is always something I've tried
to preserve in this dog-eat-dog world. [289]
Margaret Smith Court

Legends and Legacies - they go together. Margaret Court is a tennis legend and an even greater Australian legend whose legacy is cemented on playing surfaces that bear her name.

Born 16 July 1942, in Albery, Australia, Margaret Smith Court has won more Grand Slam tennis championships than any woman alive - 62 in all: 24 singles, 19 women's doubles and 19 mixed doubles. In 1970 she achieved the Grand Slam of tennis by winning the Australian Open, French Open, U.S. Open and Wimbledon - the four major Grand Slam competitions of a calendar year. Between 1960 and 1966, she won seven straight Australian Open singles titles. Such a record is, unequivocally, the indelible legacy of a legitimate legend.[290]

All champions have legacies, but not all champions have grace, and it is the combination of athletic legacy and personal grace that create true championship greatness. Margaret Court had both, and in that regard, even if her records are broken, she will always be the Jeweled Crown of the Tennis Court.

As a result of her exceptional competitive skills, championship record, personal character - expressive of integrity, respect and humility - and her notable role- model persona, Margaret Court, nicknamed "The Arm" by fellow tennis great Billy Jean King,[291] was honored by her country in 2003 as a national icon and luminary, her image commemorated on two Australian postage stamps: one image being a portrait; the other, an action shot. Male Australian tennis legend, Rod Laver, was also so honored. Each was presented with 24 carat gold replicas of their stamps.[292]

Florence Griffith Joyner: Flo-Jo
Sport: Track

I pray hard, work hard and leave the rest to God.[293]

Flo-Jo

Fast . . . very fast . . . and flashy, oozing an exotic beauty and glamorous flamboyance reserved generally for Hollywood starlets. That was Flo-Jo, Florence Griffith Joyner - the fastest woman alive.

Born the seventh of eleven children in the Watts section of Los Angeles, California, on 21 December 1959, Griffith Joyner set world speed records in the 100 and 200 meter sprints that have not been equaled to this day. Both records were set in 1988. Flo-Jo's 100 meter time was 10:49 (set at the Olympic trials); her 200 meter time, 21:34 (set at the Seoul Olympics). The closest times to her 100 meter and 200 meter efforts were registered by Marion Jones in 1998 who turned in a 10.65 clocking in the 100 and a 21:62 in the 200 in races run at an elevation in excess of 1000 meters.[294]

King

The world's fastest woman - glamorous, flamboyant, different and distant - was a competitor not without controversy. In the 1984 Olympics in Los Angeles, she won a silver medal in the 200 meters. Then, four years later, came a transformation of the chiseled-muscle variety . . . a metamorphosis blasting her race times into orbit in 1988 and into the history books, race times that have never been equaled. Flo-Jo won 3 gold medals and 1 silver at the Seoul, Korea, Olympiad and set a world record for the 200 meters. But . . . fellow athletes and the general public at large wondered, wondered if she had been using performance altering drugs, i.e., steroids. Although she denies such a claim, and never failed a drug test, her muscular physique, history-making/time-shattering performance and abrupt retirement following the Olympic Games in 1988 with the advent of random drug testing, made her a target for skeptics and created a controversy surrounding her athletic performance which, like her world record times, still exist today.[295]

Tragically, Flo-Jo died in her sleep of an apparent heart attack at the young age of only 38 on 21 September 1998, in Orange County, California. Two years earlier in 1996, she suffered a heart seizure while on a flight to St. Louis. To be sure, it was a sad and tragic day for sports.

Flo-Jo's legacy is not one just of six-inch nails, flamboyant body suits, dazzling speed, world records, Olympic Gold and Silver medals and competitive controversy, it is also one of human compassion and outreach. She founded the non-profit Florence Griffith Joyner Youth Foundation to help disadvantaged youth. She was also an author of children's books, a poet, fashion designer and served as co-chair of the President's Council on Physical Fitness and Sports. Too, Flo-Jo was admired by countless people, as well as serving as a role model and inspiration for young children.[296]

Jackie Joyner Kersee
Sport: Track & Field

Once I leave this earth, I know I've done something that will continue to help others.[297]

The medals don't mean anything and the glory doesn't last. It's all about your happiness. The rewards are going to come, but my happiness is just loving the sport and having fun performing.[298]
Jackie Joyner Kersee

How interesting it would be to be a fly on the wall, over-hearing a conversation between Babe Didrikson Zaharias and Jackie Joyner Kersee. Imagine the talk the two of them would have about athletics, women in sports, event specificity technique, training methodology; psychological, dietary and physical conditioning regimens, achievement, diversity in sport, name, fame, notoriety, success, societal pressures, triumph, failure and defeat. Why? Because these two remarkable women - Babe Didrikson and Jackie Joyner Kersee - are arguably the two greatest female athletes of the Twentieth Century.

In fact, Joyner-Kersee became inspired to ply her athletic wares in multiple events after she saw a television movie about the diversified, accomplished and world renown Babe Didrikson in 1975.[299] The movie must have cast its magic spell because in 1986, Jackie Joyner-Kersee

132

broke the 7,000 point barrier in the heptathlon at the Goodwill Games in Moscow, making her the first woman to hold a multi-event record since Babe Didrikson[300] won five of eight events in the 1932 AAU Olympic trials and then went on to win 2 gold medals while breaking her own world records in the javelin and 80 meter hurdles at the 1932 Los Angeles Olympic Games. She also won a silver medal in the high jump.

Admittedly, Jackie was inspired by the Babe, which begs the question: "Can the seed be greater than its source?" What would have happened had JJK never seen a movie of Babe Didrikson, or even if Didrikson had never lived? And who knows, from a metaphysical standpoint, maybe Jackie Joyner Kersee is the reincarnation of Babe Didrikson? Interesting thought. Cosmic energy does have a way of encircling itself. Babe Didrikson died in Galveston, Texas, on 27 September 1956; Jacqueline Joyner was born on 3 March 1962,[301] only five years later. Hmmm. . .

Regardless of the incarnation scenario, Jackie Joyner-Kersee, sister-in-law to Flo-Jo (Florence Griffith Joyner married Jackie's brother), was phenomenally versatile as an athlete. Beginning as a dancer and cheerleader in her early years,[302] she began expanding her talents in her teenage years, winning four consecutive National Junior Pentathlon Championships, the first at age 14. She also played volleyball in high school but excelled so much in basketball that she accepted a scholarship to UCLA where she not only earned All-American honors as a Bruins starter, but eventually married her basketball coach, Bob Kersee, who, seeing her extreme and versatile athletic gifts, encouraged her to train for multiple-event contests, which, as history declares emphatically, she did.

The Age of the Female II: Heroines of the Shift

Jackie competed in an unbelievable four Olympic Games. Her main event was the heptathlon, a consecutive two day macro event featuring 7 micro events in the following order: Day 1 - 100 meter hurdles; high jump; shot put; 200 meters; Day 2 - long jump; javelin; 800 meters. It is in this event in which Joyner-Kersee was poignantly dominant - maintaining the six best performances in hepthalon history.

Her Olympic record: 1984 - Los Angeles (silver medal in the hepthalon); 1988 - Seoul, South Korea (gold medal in the heptathlon and long jump); 1992 - Barcelona, Spain (gold in heptathlon; bronze in the long jump) and 1996 in Atlanta (bronze in long jump). In all, she won 3 gold, 1 silver and 2 bronze medals during the Olympic Games.[303]

Jackie Joyner-Kersee has received many awards, including the 1985 Broderick Cup as outstanding collegiate woman athlete; the James E. Sullivan Award in 1986 and the Jesse Owens Award in 1986 and '87. She was named Associated Press Female Athlete of the Year in 1987, and became the first woman to win The Sporting News Man of the Year Award in 1988.[304] *Sports Illustrated for Women* honored Jackie Joyner Kersee and her exceptional, profound talent by recognizing her as the Greatest Female Athlete of the 20th Century.[305]

The Age of the Female II: Heroines of the Shift

CHAPTER FOUR

NOTABLE YIN

Excellence and eminence;
benevolence and brilliance;
adulation, approbation rising.
Notable Yin extends her wings,
sings her songs and soars
into skies which actualize,
recognize, and eulogize
accomplishments renown.
In every field she has sealed
records of her touch;
on every road she has bestowed
gifts dispensing much
of the heart which ticks within her.
It is now her time to soar the skies;
for a world in time and space
to realize with its own eyes
the majesty of her race.

King

With the dawning of The Age of the Female and the rise of the Yin, there have been a plethora of women who deserve recognition and applause. Their accomplishments have been and continue to be reflected in every aspect of society. Their attainments are immense; not token. Their rise continuous; not broken. Their sacrifice and service, extraordinary; not ordinary . . . by any stretch of the imagination and, to be sure, their achievements have been conspicuously credible, laudable, applaudable, memorable, undeniable and irrefutable.

However, as with 'Athletic Yin,' the pages of this work could not hold the numbers of those distinguished women worthy of note. Many have been mentioned in previous chapters. A few others have been selected here to represent the many, but their selection here in no way diminishes or minimizes those who are not included here. The rise of the female onto the world stage has been a remarkable and prodigious event in world history, and the catalogue of women of all ages who have made a contribution to the promotion of female presence and prominence in the amphitheater of earth is far too expansive to include within the confines of this work. Nonetheless, the gifts and grants of time, effort, thought, heart, sweat, blood, fears, tears, hopes, dreams and energies of everyone associated with the rise and expansion of Yin energy are all deeply appreciated and acknowledged en masse and in main.

Anne Frank
Author

Whoever is happy will make others happy too.
He who has courage and faith will never
perish in misery! [306]
Anne Frank

Imagine this: prisoners - women, children, old men - being stuffed into a room like sardines so tightly and in such quantity that when they are collectively murdered by gas, their corpses, by virtue of their bodies being crammed, packed and stacked so tightly together, cannot collapse to the floor but are left in a standing position, shoulder to shoulder, dead. Such a scenario brings a new, grim, and ghastly meaning to the phrase 'dead on your feet.'

Imagine lifeless, decaying corpses, or, more precisely, flesh covered skeletons, being stacked upon one another in humongous heaps like worthless logs waiting their individual turn to be summarily thrown into an oven and incinerated by fire, the stench of their burning flesh wafting for miles through the countryside. Such a disgusting image changes the phrase 'fresh air' to 'flesh air.'

Imagine, too, having armed guards take you and your father off to the side of a road, positioning him on his knees, placing the barrel of a pistol at the back of his head, summarily squeezing the trigger and shooting him to death at point blank range and . . . in your presence. Then, coldly and heartlessly, having these conscienceless guards escort you away at gunpoint, bequeathing your father's body, not to you or his loved ones, but to insects, flies, worms, birds, water, wind and the

King

138

elements to become nothing more than a nameless, putrefying carcass rotting away in some forgotten field - all this with neither the dignity nor the respect of a proper burial.

These sad, tragic and heinous acts of senseless, cold-blooded murder were all realities of the holocaust - the mass destruction of human (mostly Jewish) life perpetrated by the villainous, iniquitous and egomaniacal Adolf Hitler during World War II. This was a time where innocence was truly plagued by the nefarious nescience of nazi nemesis. These were the truculent times of a young Jewish girl named Anne Frank, times which ended her own life at the sweet and tender age of sixteen.

The second daughter of Otto and Edith Frank, Anneliese Marie was born on 12 June 1929 in Frankfurt, Germany. She had an older sister by three years, Margot. The Franks were a family which led a frightful life, a life shared by far too many people in those times in that part of the world; a life also ending far too tragically, but . . . a life that would leave a legacy of remembrance to a world which would, hopefully, never forget the holocaust and man's vicious display of his inhumanity to himself.

With the ever-expanding tyranny of Nazi rule, the Frank family fled to Amsterdam in the Netherlands in 1933. Unfortunately, Hitler's tentacles kept creeping outward, eventually infesting Amsterdam with their poisonous and deadly grip.[307] Escape from the claws of the Third Reich had only been temporary for the Franks.

While living in Amsterdam and on the occasion of her thirteenth birthday, the 12th of June 1942, Anne Frank was given a diary by her parents in appreciation for her love of writing. It was a gift which would actually to be given to the world years later, but no one at the time, not even Anne, knew of its future legacy. Of her passion for writing she says: "I want to write, but more than that, I want to bring out all kinds of things that lie buried deep in my heart."[308]

This is an interesting quote because Anne Frank's Lifepath, the script of her life, was a 3 - the vibration of words, language, communication and self-expression (12 June 1929 > 1 + 2 + 6 + 1 + 9 + 2 + 9 = 30 > 3 + 0 = 3). Her Simple Expression (Anneliese Marie Frank) was a 9, the energy of expansion, broadcasting, the macrocosm and public spotlight. When added together these made her Simple Performance/Experience, the reality of her life also a 3 (3 Lifepath + 9 Expression = 12 > 1 + 2 = 3). Therefore, communication and public exposure were major themes of Anne Frank's destiny.

Three short weeks after the receipt of her parent's gift, the Franks were forced into hiding on the 6th of July 1942, voluntarily incarcerating themselves in the attic of their father's business. In an effort to avoid Nazi detection, subsequent imprisonment in a concentration camp and possible death, they lived secretly and fearfully for twenty-five months within the confines of their secret hideaway.[309]

In that span of two years, Anne Frank wrote in her diary which she called 'Kitty.' In epistolary (letter) form, the entry of her Diary's first page reads: " I hope I shall be able to confide in you completely, as I have never been able to do in anyone before, and I hope that you will be a great support and comfort to me."[310] Subsequent pages written through the next twenty-five months depicted the nightmare reality of the eight people living secretly in the tiny attic at Prinsengracht 263, Amsterdam. In her diary Anne reveals her fears, dreams, hopes and feelings of a young teenage girl approaching womanhood - a phase of life which destiny would deny her.

King

140

In one of her entries Anne's youthful and innocent optimism shines: "I still believe, in spite of everything, that people are still truly good at heart." But in moments of doubt and rage she writes: "I simply can't build up my hopes on a foundation consisting of confusion, misery and death." [311] Needless to say, the tender, young and innocent life of Anne Frank was fraught with fear and uncertainty; a tender, young and innocent life unknown to many children of her age in today's world.

Eventually, the family and their hiding place were betrayed. Anne's last diary entry was on the 1st of August, 1944, a universal 9 day depicting endings, conclusions and finalizations ($1 + 8 + 1 + 9 + 4 + 4 = 27 > 2 + 7 = 9$) which also incorporated a 9 First Pinnacle (1 August $= 1 + 8 = 9$). This final entry occurred three days before the family's arrest by the Nazis on the 4th of August. Fortunately, the diary escaped detection. After all, it had no monetary value to the Germans. It would be rediscovered after the war, its precious messages left to history and all mankind.

The Frank family members were taken away and dispersed after their arrest. Anne's mother, Edith, died in 1945 in the killing camp of Auschwitz-Birkenau.[312] Anne and her older sister, Margot, were transferred from the Dutch concentration camp, Westerbork, to Bergen-Belsen where Margot died of typhus in 1945, just weeks before Anne succumbed to the same disease at the tender, innocent age of sixteen.

Their father, Otto, survived until 1980 and devoted the remainder of his life to sharing his daughter's diary with the world.[313] Eventually translated into some 60 languages, the diary first appeared in 1947 as *Het Achterhuis* (The House Behind). In 1952 its English translation appeared under the title, *The Diary of a Young Girl.* Its final metamorphosis was *The Diary of Anne Frank*, being dramatized for the theater in 1956 and then into film form in 1959 where its fame and fortune were found.[314]

The story of Anne Frank is important because it highlights perhaps the most heinous, insidious and tragic event of the Twentieth Century - the Holocaust. Had this innocent young girl not had a passion for writing and sharing her thoughts, the world would have been denied a more complete 'knowing' of the scope of its horror. Although young, Anne Frank's gift to the world was immense, and she is, without question, one of the most notable and unforgettable women of the Twentieth Century.

Barbara Walters
Television Journalist

I was the kind nobody thought could make it.
I had a funny Boston accent.
I couldn't pronounce my R's.
I wasn't a beauty. [315]

Notwithstanding her own thoughts about others thinking she couldn't 'make it,' or feelings of her own personal peculiarities, Barbara Walters did make it, and big doesn't come close to either describing her professional success or the impact she has had on literally billions of people the world over . . . for decades.

Born on 25 September 1931, Barbara Walters' destiny was saturated in 3 energy - the energy of communication. Her Lifepath, the script of her life, is not only a 3, but her Grand Pinnacle (the core of her life) and her Crown Pinnacle (her 4th and last) are also 3s. Her Grand Challenge and Crown Challenge are both 2s. In effect, the destiny of Barbara Walters was indelibly concentrated in 'communication with others,' a destiny which has earned her the esteemed title "First Lady of Television."[316]

It is literally impossible to calculate the immense effect Barbara Walters has had on people in general and females in particular during the course of her professional life. Before 1976, nightly network television news was anchored exclusively by men. Without a doubt, up until then, prime time news television was a man's world, a yang world. However, because of her prior television success and astute communicative ability, Walters was offered a ground-breaking, record-setting, million dollar salary-busting-position as co-anchor of ABC News with Harry Reasoner in 1976. It was a huge stride forward for females in network television.

The format, however, did not enjoy smooth sailing, was controversial, and subsequently abandoned after two years. However, the door to male-only primetime news broadcasting was irrevocably closed. Dusk had sat on the yang day. The guard had changed. History was made. Yin had risen. Without a doubt, it was no longer a man's world, a yang world. It was now a man/woman world; a yang/yin world, a world where the general public became recipients of male and female energy from a major television news format, a world reflecting balance in communication and communicators, a world made possible by one Barbara Walters.[317] The broadcast female media door had been opened. Destiny served.

The Age of the Female II: Heroines of the Shift

143

Walters' contract with ABC News was truly ground-breaking, but her gifts were, frankly, more expansive than a news format could offer or contain. Within the framework of her own "Barbara Walters Specials" which began in 1976,[318] Walters has interviewed many of the most interesting and powerful people on earth - a statement offering a cloudless, crystalline commentary of her own power, a power so based in personal integrity that world leaders obviously felt comfortable in speaking with and being interviewed by her.

For example, in 1977 Walters made journalism history when she arranged a joint interview between Israel's Prime Minister Menachem Begin and Egypt's President Anwar Sadat - the first ever. Another first was her interview with Fidel Castro, President of Cuba. Walters has also interviewed every American President since Richard Nixon, Colin Powell (former United States Chairman of the Joint Chiefs of Staff and Secretary of State under George Bush Jr.), Russia's Boris Yeltsin, China's Premier Jiang Zemin, Great Britain's former Prime Minister Margaret Thatcher, India's Indira Ghandi, Jordan's King Hussein, Moammar Qaddafi, the Shah of Iran, and such movie greats as Bette Davis, Sir Laurence Olivier, Bing Crosby, John Wayne, Katherine Hepburn, Audrey Hepburn, Elizabeth Taylor, Harrison Ford, Barbara Streisand, Tom Cruise, Tom Hanks and Julia Roberts, just to name a few.[319] With such an extraordinary cavalcade of world famous personalities giving permission to be interviewed by her, one has to wonder as to the scope and dimension of Walters' personal power and to respect it, honor it, applaud it. Who else in the journalism world can lay claim to having interviewed such a distinguished list of luminaries and dignitaries?

One may ask, "What is Walters' interviewing secret?" Here's what she says: "Wait for those unguarded moments. Relax the mood and, like the child dropping off to sleep, the subject often reveals his truest self." Could this be one of the secrets to her success? Most likely. However, in relation to personal attainment, Walters' says, "One may walk over the highest mountain one step at a time"[320] - an effective philosophy from one of the most effective journalists of all time.

Barbara Walters' list of achievements is as extraordinary as her talent. Included are: 1. inducted into the Academy of Television Arts and Sciences' Hall of Fame "for being acknowledged worldwide as one of television's most respected interviewers and journalists," 1990; 2. honored with the Lowell Thomas Award for a career in journalism excellence by Marist College, 1990; 3. honored by the Overseas Press Club with their highest award, the President's Award, 1988; 4. saluted by the American Museum of the Moving Image, March 19, 1992; 5. Lifetime Achievement Award, International Women's Media Foundation, 1991; 6. Lifetime Achievement Award, Women's Project and Productions, 1993; 7. honored by the Museum of Television & Radio for her contributions to broadcast journalism, 1996; and 8. the "Muse" Award from New York Women in Film and Television, 1997. Ms. Walters is the recipient of honorary doctoral degrees from Ohio State University, Temple University, Marymount College, Wheaton College, Hofstra University, and Ben-Gurion University in Jerusalem. Barbara Walters has also been entrepreneurial. She is co-owner, co-executive producer and a co-host on "The View," ABC's highest rated show in the 11:00 a.m.-12:00 noon time period since the 1993-94 season.[321]

The Age of the Female II: Heroines of the Shift

Eleanor Roosevelt
First Lady of the World

What is to give light must endure the burning. [322]

Do what you feel in your heart to be right -
for you'll be criticized anyway. You'll be damned if you do,
and damned if you don't. [323]

By all accounts, Eleanor Roosevelt was not only one of the most influential women of the 1900s, she was also one of the greatest individuals of the Twentieth Century. Her stature, grace, intelligence, fortitude, wisdom, support for her husband, Franklin Delano Roosevelt (FDR), the 32nd President of the United States, and her indefatigable service to promote human rights within the world community caused United States President Harry S. Truman (1945 to 1953) to regard and honor Eleanor Roosevelt as the "First Lady of the World."[324]

Born Anna Eleanor Roosevelt in New York City on 11 October 1884 to parents Anna Hall and Elliott Roosevelt, younger brother of Teddy Roosevelt, the 26th President of the United States, Eleanor was born into a destiny which would solidify her as a great humanitarian and superlative human being.[325]

Eleanor's parents both died when she was quite young - her mother in 1892 when she was eight and her father two years later in 1894 when she was ten. Having lived with her maternal grandmother, Eleanor journeyed to England to go to school. Upon her return, she eventually married her distant cousin, FDR, in 1905. Her uncle, President

Theodore "Teddy" Roosevelt of Rough Rider fame (1901 to 1909), gave the bride, his niece, away.[326]

It is interesting that Eleanor was born a Roosevelt and married a Roosevelt. Thus, her maiden name and married name were obviously identical. It is also interesting that both her uncle and cousin/husband were Presidents of the United States. Thus, in many ways she, more than most females who become wives of presidents, was encapsulated in the aura of a First Lady from a very early age. By the time she entered the White House in 1933 with the election of her husband as President, she had a keen understanding of her role, her official duties and her power.

Throughout FDR's political life, from his first successful campaign in 1928 through two terms as President of the United States and through his affliction with polio, Eleanor dedicated her life to his purposes, becoming his eyes, ears, trusted reporter and confidant. She would even hold press conferences, breaking former precedents. She traveled extensively, gave lectures, participated in radio broadcasts, and openly expressed her opinions in a daily syndicated newspaper column entitled, "My Day." All of this made her a political target for her adversaries, but her sincerity of purpose, personal integrity and graciousness endeared her to many heads of state and people in general around the world. In effect, she lived a quote which she authored at the tender age of only fourteen: "...No matter how plain a woman may be, if truth and loyalty are stamped upon her face, all will be attracted to her...."[327] It certainly seems she took a thought from the Bard himself: "This above all, to thine own self be true and it must follow as the night the day, thou canst' not then be false to any man."(William Shakespeare: *Hamlet,* Act I: Scene 3).

The Age of the Female II: Heroines of the Shift

During her life, Eleanor Roosevelt's reputation expanded to reflect the sentiments of her heart. She was one of those rare, radiant, illuminating human beings who walked her talk. She has many marvelous quotes which are educational as well as inspirational. One of her favorite quotes was: "You get more joy out of the giving to others, and should put a good deal of thought into the happiness you are able to give."[328] Other quotations from her rich treasure chest of wisdom are:

Only a man's character is the real criterion of worth.

When you cease to make a contribution, you begin to die.

Justice cannot be for one side alone, but must be for both.

It is not fair to ask of others what you are not willing to do yourself.

We are afraid to care too much, for fear that the other person does not care at all.

It isn't enough to talk about peace. One must believe in it. And it isn't enough to believe in it. One must work at it.

We gain strength, and courage and confidence by each experience in which we really stop to look fear in the face . . . we must do that which we think we cannot.[329]

In corroboration of her compassion, understanding and genuine character, American statesman and politician Adlai Stevenson, once honored Eleanor Roosevelt by saying, "She would rather light a candle than curse the darkness," a quote she used herself many times.[330]

Notwithstanding her role as First Lady and devoted wife to her husband, Eleanor Roosevelt's greatest legacy was her dedication and relentless work with the United Nations on the Universal Declaration of Human Rights. Undoubtedly, she was the UN's most influential proponent in this regard. Her leadership led to the composition of the Declaration which has endured as a universally accepted standard of achievement for all nations.[331] In respect for her work on its behalf, as well as offering a statement which parallels the positive energy of the Age of the Female, the Age of Others - the 2nd Millennium in which we of planet earth are all now an integral part - it is presented below.

Interestingly, the Declaration of Human Rights was adopted on the 10th of December 1948. This date, numerologically, maintains a Specific Lifepath cipher of 44/8 - a master number of intense structural organization, leadership and power (10 + 12 [December] + 22 [1948 in reduction] = 44 > 8 or 44/8).

Universal Declaration of Human Rights

On 10 December 1948, the General Assembly of the United Nations adopted and proclaimed the Universal Declaration of Human Rights. Following this historic act, the Assembly called upon all Member countries to publicize the text of the Declaration and "to cause it to be disseminated, displayed, read and expounded principally in schools and other educational institutions, without distinction based on the political status of countries or territories."

Preamble

Whereas recognition of the inherent dignity and of the equal and inalienable rights of all members of the human family is the foundation of freedom, justice and peace in the world,

Whereas disregard and contempt for human rights have resulted in barbarous acts which have outraged the conscience of mankind, and the advent of a world in which human beings shall enjoy freedom of speech and belief and freedom from fear and want has been proclaimed as the highest aspiration of the common people,

Whereas it is essential, if man is not to be compelled to have recourse, as a last resort, to rebellion against tyranny and oppression, that human rights should be protected by the rule of law,

Whereas it is essential to promote the development of friendly relations between nations,

Whereas the peoples of the United Nations have in the Charter reaffirmed their faith in fundamental human rights, in the dignity and worth of the human person and in the equal rights of men and women and have determined to promote social progress and better standards of life in larger freedom,

Whereas Member States have pledged themselves to achieve, in co-operation with the United Nations, the promotion of universal respect for and observance of human rights and fundamental freedoms,

Whereas a common understanding of these rights and freedoms is of the greatest importance for the full realization of this pledge,

Now, therefore, the General Assembly proclaims this Universal Declaration of Human Rights as a common standard of achievement for all peoples and all nations, to the end that every individual and every organ of society, keeping this Declaration constantly in mind, shall strive by teaching and education to promote respect for these rights and freedoms and by progressive measures, national and international, to secure their universal and effective recognition and observance, both among the peoples of Member States themselves and among the peoples of territories under their jurisdiction.

Article 1.

All human beings are born free and equal in dignity and rights. They are endowed with reason and conscience and should act towards one another in a spirit of brotherhood.

Article 2.

Everyone is entitled to all the rights and freedoms set forth in this Declaration, without distinction of any kind, such as race, colour, sex, language, religion, political or other opinion, national or social origin, property, birth or other status. Furthermore, no distinction shall be made on the basis of the political, jurisdictional or international status of the country or territory to which a person belongs, whether it be independent, trust, non-self-governing or under any other limitation of sovereignty.

Article 3.

Everyone has the right to life, liberty and security of person.

Article 4.

No one shall be held in slavery or servitude; slavery and the slave trade shall be prohibited in all their forms.

Article 5.

No one shall be subjected to torture or to cruel, inhuman or degrading treatment or punishment.

Article 6.

Everyone has the right to recognition everywhere as a person before the law.

Article 7.

All are equal before the law and are entitled without any discrimination to equal protection of the law. All are entitled to equal protection against any discrimination in violation of this Declaration and against any incitement to such discrimination.

Article 8.

Everyone has the right to an effective remedy by the competent national tribunals for acts violating the fundamental rights granted him by the constitution or by law.

Article 9.

No one shall be subjected to arbitrary arrest, detention or exile.

Article 10.

Everyone is entitled in full equality to a fair and public hearing by an independent and impartial tribunal, in the determination of his rights and obligations and of any criminal charge against him.

Article 11.

(1) Everyone charged with a penal offence has the right to be presumed innocent until proved guilty according to law in a public trial at which he has had all the guarantees necessary for his defence.

(2) No one shall be held guilty of any penal offence on account of any act or omission which did not constitute a penal offence, under national or international law, at the time when it was   committed. Nor shall a heavier penalty be imposed than the one that was applicable at the time the penal offence was committed.

King

Article 12.

No one shall be subjected to arbitrary interference with his privacy, family, home or correspondence, nor to attacks upon his honour and reputation. Everyone has the right to the protection of the law against such interference or attacks.

Article 13.

(1) Everyone has the right to freedom of movement and residence within the borders of each state.

(2) Everyone has the right to leave any country, including his own, and to return to his country.

Article 14.

(1) Everyone has the right to seek and to enjoy in other countries asylum from persecution.

(2) This right may not be invoked in the case of prosecutions genuinely arising from non-political crimes or from acts contrary to the purposes and principles of the United Nations.

Article 15.

(1) Everyone has the right to a nationality.

(2) No one shall be arbitrarily deprived of his nationality nor denied the right to change his nationality.

Article 16.

(1) Men and women of full age, without any limitation due to race, nationality or religion, have the right to marry and to found a family. They are entitled to equal rights as to marriage, during marriage and at its dissolution.

(2) Marriage shall be entered into only with the free and full consent of the intending spouses.

(3) The family is the natural and fundamental group unit of society and is entitled to protection by society and the State.

Article 17.

(1) Everyone has the right to own property alone as well as in association with others.

(2) No one shall be arbitrarily deprived of his property.

Article 18.

Everyone has the right to freedom of thought, conscience and religion; this right includes freedom to change his religion or belief, and freedom, either alone or in community with others and in public or private, to manifest his religion or belief in teaching, practice, worship and observance.

Article 19.

Everyone has the right to freedom of opinion and expression; this right includes freedom to hold opinions without interference and to seek, receive and impart information and ideas through any media and regardless of frontiers.

Article 20.

(1) Everyone has the right to freedom of peaceful assembly and association.

(2) No one may be compelled to belong to an association.

Article 21.

(1) Everyone has the right to take part in the government of his country, directly or through freely chosen representatives.

(2) Everyone has the right of equal access to public service in his country.

(3) The will of the people shall be the basis of the authority of government; this will shall be expressed in periodic and genuine

elections which shall be by universal and equal suffrage and shall be held by secret vote or by equivalent free voting procedures.

Article 22.

Everyone, as a member of society, has the right to social security and is entitled to realization, through national effort and international co-operation and in accordance with the organization and resources of each State, of the economic, social and cultural rights indispensable for his dignity and the free development of his personality.

Article 23.

(1) Everyone has the right to work, to free choice of employment, to just and favourable conditions of work and to protection against unemployment.

(2) Everyone, without any discrimination, has the right to equal pay for equal work.

(3) Everyone who works has the right to just and favourable remuneration ensuring for himself and his family an existence worthy of human dignity, and supplemented, if necessary, by other means of social protection.

(4) Everyone has the right to form and to join trade unions for the protection of his interests.

Article 24.

Everyone has the right to rest and leisure, including reasonable limitation of working hours and periodic holidays with pay.

Article 25.

(1) Everyone has the right to a standard of living adequate for the health and well-being of himself and of his family, including food, clothing, housing and medical care and necessary social services, and the right to security in the event of unemployment, sickness, disability, widowhood, old age orother lack of livelihood in circumstances beyond his control.

(2) Motherhood and childhood are entitled to special care and assistance. All children, whether born in or out of wedlock, shall enjoy the same social protection.

Article 26.

(1) Everyone has the right to education. Education shall be free, at least in the elementary and fundamental stages. Elementary education shall be compulsory. Technical and professional education shall be made generally available and higher education shall be equally accessible to all on the basis of merit.

(2) Education shall be directed to the full development of the human personality and to the strengthening of respect for human rights and fundamental freedoms. It shall promote understanding, tolerance and friendship among all nations, racial or religious groups, and shall further the activities of the United Nations for the maintenance of peace.

(3) Parents have a prior right to choose the kind of education that shall be given to their children.

Article 27.

(1) Everyone has the right freely to participate in the cultural life of the community, to enjoy the arts and to share in scientific advancement and its benefits.

(2) Everyone has the right to the protection of the moral and material interests resulting from any scientific, literary or artistic production of which he is the author.

Article 28.

Everyone is entitled to a social and international order in which the rights and freedoms set forth in this Declaration can be fully realized.

Article 29.

(1) Everyone has duties to the community in which alone the free and full development of his personality is possible.

(2) In the exercise of his rights and freedoms, everyone shall be subject only to such limitations as are determined by law solely for the purpose of securing due recognition and respect for the rights and freedoms of others and of meeting the just requirements of morality, public order and the general welfare in a democratic society.

(3) These rights and freedoms may in no case be exercised contrary to the purposes and principles of the United Nations.

Article 30.

Nothing in this Declaration may be interpreted as implying for any State, group or person any right to engage in any activity or to perform any act aimed at the destruction of any of the rights and freedoms set forth herein.[332]

Elisabeth Kubler-Ross
Humanitarian

Learn to get in touch with the silence within yourself
and know that everything in this life has a purpose.[333]
Elisabeth Kubler-Ross

To every day there is a night. To every life there is a death. Unfortunately, most of us go on living day by day never thinking of the night to come, the hour of our death to come; never considering how we will deal with such an inevitable transition. In a way, we shun the reality of death, thinking that if we bury our heads in the sand it will just go away and we will never have to prepare for it nor confront it - in ourselves or in others. Elisabeth Kubler-Ross, stubborn and ornery by fond description of those closest to her, changed our perception of life and death, especially death.[334]

Born in Zurich, Switzerland, one of triplets, Elisabeth Kubler graduated from the University of Zurich with a medical degree in 1957.[335] While attending to her undergraduate studies, she met, fell in love with and eventually married Emanuel Ross. They moved to the United States in 1958. Shocked by how dying patients were treated as 'untouchables' while working as a resident in New York hospitals, Kubler-Ross set out on a course of action which would change the way the world viewed death and the dying. In speaking of the dying she states: "They were shunned and abused, nobody was honest with them."[336]

Her first book, "On Death and Dying" in 1969 became an international best seller and compensated her with a worldwide reputation and a household name.[337] Says Kubler-Ross, "My goal was to break through the layer of professional denial that prohibited patients from airing their inner-most concerns." For decades she devoted her life to the plight of the dying, speaking to standing-room only audiences and writing over twenty books on the subject which made her an internationally renowned author.[338]

Undoubtedly, the work of Elisabeth Kubler-Ross raised the awareness of the world in relation to the dusk of life. To be sure, for all of us who possess a heartbeat, death is our future, whether we acknowledge such a reality or not. Kubler-Ross made us aware of that dusky future through the capacity of doctor, author, teacher, lecturer, instructor, director.

Elisabeth Kubler-Ross has authored over twenty books in her chosen field. She has been awarded over twenty honorary doctoral degrees from major educational institutions in the fields of science, laws, humanities, humane letters, humane science, pedagogy and divinity. Among her many awards are: One Hundred Most Important Thinkers of the Century, Time Magazine, 1999; One Hundred Most Important Books of the Century, New York Public Library; Outstanding Achievement, World Institute of Achievement, 1986; Woman of the Decade, Ladies Home Journal, 1979; Woman of the Year, Ladies Home Journal, 1977; Teilhard Prize, Teilhard Foundation, 1981; Lifetime Achievement, Southern Birmingham College, 1995; Service to Mankind Award, Southwest Sertoma Club, Kansas City, Missouri, 1977; Living Legacy Award, Women's International Center, La Jolla, California, 1984; Modern Samaritan Award, 1976; Life Fellow, John F. Kennedy Library, 1987; Inclusion in: The World Who's Who of Women, International Biographical Centre, Cambridge,

England, 1986; Ideal Citizen Award, Chicago, Illinois, 1977; Humanitarian Award, International Association of Cancer Victims and Friends, Inc., Solano Beach, California, 1977.[339]

Golda Meir
Statesman

Trust yourself. Create the kind of self
that you will be happy to live with all your life.
Make the most of yourself by fanning the tiny,
inner sparks of possibility into flames of achievement.[340]
Golda Meir

Golda Meir was born on 3 May 1898 in Kyyiv, Russia (now the Ukraine).[341] Her original name has been given as Golda Mabovitch[342] and Goldie Mobovitz. In 1956 she Hebraized her surname to Meir.[343] Regardless of spelling, the name of Golda Meir has become synonymous with commitment to her land, her cause, and her people. She has been referred to as the paragon of human dedication.[344]

Meir's father immigrated in 1905 from Russia to the United States. Settling in Milwaukee, Wisconsin, his family joined him a year later. During her teenage years, Meir became a Zionist, her interest devoted to building a homeland for Jews. She attended Milwaukee Teachers College, married Morris Meyerson in 1917, and in 1921 she and her husband immigrated to Palestine (now Israel) where she became active in Zionist affairs.

During her political life, Meir served in several Zionist organizations in the United States, Europe and Palestine. In 1948 she was a signer of the proclamation for the independence of Israel. In the years 1948 and 1949 she served as her country's first minister to the USSR and was elected to the first Knesset (parliament of Israel) in 1949. In that same year she was also named Minister of Labor and Social Insurance. In 1956 she became Minister of Foreign Affairs, a post she held until 1966. Her next assignment was Secretary-General of the Mapai Party and the United Israel Labor Party from 1966 to 1968. Then in 1969 she became Prime Minister of Israel and held that post until her resignation in 1974.[345]

In becoming Israel's Prime Minister, Golda Meir became only the third female Prime Minister in history. The first was Sirimavo Bandaranaike of Sri Lanka (1960-1965; 1970-1977) and the second, Indira Ghandi of India (1966-1977; 1980-1984).[346]

During her esteemed service as Prime Minister, one of Meir's passions was working with agricultural and urban planning programs between Africa and her country. It was a well-known fact that her greatest concern was for her people, ensuring their protection and security.[347]

If there were a major event marking her administration, it was the Yom Kippur War which erupted on 6 October 1973. Massive Egyptian and Syrian assaults caught Israel off guard. Although Israeli forces were able to recover and ultimately push back the assault, the war was considered a diplomatic and military failure. Meir was criticized for Israel's lack of preparedness. Subsequently, she resigned amid the controversy in 1974 in favor of Yitzhak Rabin.[348]

What Golda Meir did, she did for people. Her dedication to them and her country is legendary. She died in December of 1978 at the age of 80 and was buried on Mount Herzl in Jerusalem.[349] Golda Meir is still deeply loved and admired, not only by those within her country but around the world.[350]

Helen Keller
Paragon of Icons

Character cannot be developed in ease and quiet.
Only through experience of trial and suffering can
the soul be strengthened, ambition inspired, and
success achieved.[351]

We could never learn to be brave and patient
if there were only joy in the world.[352]

It is axiomatic that those who have suffered the most, who have endured the most, have the most to offer. It is also apparent that those individuals exuding true substance, worth and value have been the ones most tempered, tested, wrought and bought with fire. To them, ease of life has been denied; in dis-ease they have been tried; through storms and tempests they have cried, but in triumph, unquestionably undenied.

Such was the personage of Helen Keller. Her life was extraordinary and heroic, a life so remarkable that the great American literary legend, Mark Twain said: "The two most interesting characters of the 19th century are Napoleon and Helen Keller." In his eulogy at

King

her passing (1 June 1968), Alabama Senator Lister Hill evoked the world's universal sentiments: "She will live on, one of the few, the immortal names not born to die. Her spirit will endure as long as man can read and stories can be told of the woman who showed the world there are no boundaries to courage and faith."[353]

Helen Adams Keller was born on 27 June 1880 in Tuscumbia, Alabama, in a frame cottage called "Ivy Green." For the first eighteen months of her life, she was physically whole and healthy. Then an illness struck which left her both blind and deaf. Diagnosed as brain fever, it may have been scarlet fever. Nonetheless, her sight and hearing were denied her for the rest of her 88 year life.[354]

The next seven years from infancy to childhood were difficult, to say the least. Helen was a wild and unruly child. No wonder. How difficult would it be for anyone to negotiate his or her ship of life without eyes and ears, especially when being a young child? Were each of us to close our eyes, how long and how well could we manage under such oppressive conditions? If we were to lose our hearing, separate from our eyesight, how difficult would our lives be? The greatest sensual contact we have with our environment is with our eyes. Were any of us to do without both for an hour would be difficult; a day, challenging; a year, nearly impossible; but 88 years of being blind and deaf? And then, in defiance of feeling sorry for oneself, not to spend one's life on the pity pot but make inspirational contributions to the whole of mankind leaves one speechless beyond words and tearful beyond tears to think of the immense struggle, dedication, determination, persistence, patience and unyielding spirit one must have to lift himself or herself into the position of world renowned hero or heroine, as well as international icon! Such a state is beyond the scope of what most of us are capable of thinking, let alone doing. But it was not out of the scope of Helen Keller. It was exactly within the scope of her life's destiny, a target which she hit dead in the center of the bull's eye.

On a serendipitous day in March of 1887, a day which Helen Keller would recall as "The most important day I can remember in my life," a young twenty year old graduate of the Perkins School for the Blind, Anne Mansfield Sullivan, entered the life of young Helen Adams Keller. It was the beginning of a teacher-student bond which lasted until death, itself being an event of rare and selfless devotion. It was, of course, Anne Sullivan - devoted, loyal, selfless and sacrificing - who struggled with the young and wild child, teaching her how to read and adjust to life exigencies in a world where she could neither see nor hear. The two were constant companions until Sullivan's death in 1936. Sullivan's loyalty to Keller was so powerfully immaculate that when Sullivan married John Macy in 1905, she never deserted her pupil. Keller went to live with the Macys and both husband and wife unselfishly gave their time to help with Keller's studies and activities.[355] Where is that kind of unsoiled, undefiled devotion today?

Overcoming all odds and extreme adversity, Helen Keller succeeded in life far beyond the level of most people who are not nearly so disadvantaged or impaired. Keller attended and graduated from Radcliffe College, began a writing career spanning some fifty years, writing most frequently on blindness, deafness, socialism, social issues and women's rights. The pinnacle and most famous of her works was *The Story of My Life* which was published in book form in 1902 and was eventually translated into more than fifty languages, a screenplay and movie, "Helen Keller in Her Story," a feature-length

King

164

documentary winning an Oscar in 1955 for producer Nancy Hamilton from the Academy of Motion Picture Arts and Sciences.[356] It was the Helen Keller Story which was also indirectly responsible for two other Oscars won by Anne Bancroft and Patty Duke in "The Miracle Worker" - a story of the Sullivan/Keller relationship. Other literary works by Helen Keller include: *The World I Live In*; *The Song of the Stone Wall*; *Out of the Dark*; *My Religion*; *Midstream--My Later Life*; *Peace at Eventide*; *Helen Keller in Scotland*; *Helen Keller's Journal*; *Let Us Have Faith*; *Teacher, Anne Sullivan Macy*; and *The Open Door*.

Helen Keller's list of personal friends and world figures reads like a Who's Who Of Planet Earth. She personally knew every American President from Grover Cleveland until her death, Alexander Graham Bell, Mark Twain, William James, Nehru, Charlie Chaplin, Katharine Cornell, to name a few. She traveled extensively during her rich and varied life, and between 1946 to 1957 made seven global tours, visited 35 countries and all 5 continents. At 75 years of age, she even undertook a five-month, 40,000 mile tour through Asia! Wherever she went, she spread courage and hope to millions of people, especially those devoid of physical sight. In fact, if you can believe this, she even said she was always searching for ways to help those "less fortunate than myself!" (goose bumps, chills and tears here)

One of her greatest challenges was the death of her beloved teacher, Anne Sullivan, in 1936. God did not abandon Keller. Polly Thomson assumed the task of assisting Helen until she (Thomson) died in 1960. She was followed by Mrs. Winfred Corbally, a nurse-companion, who served Keller until Keller's final days and remarkable life came to an end.

Awards of distinction for this legendary person and great woman are too numerous to mention, as one could well imagine. Here are a few: Presidential Medal of Freedom (America's highest civilian honor); America's Award for Inter-American Unity; Gold Medal Award from the National Institute of Social Sciences; the National Humanitarian Award from Variety Clubs International; Brazil's Order of the Southern Cross; Japan's Sacred Treasure; Philippines' Golden Heart; Lebanon's Gold Medal of Merit; inductee into the National Institute of Arts and Letters; Chevalier of the French Legion of Honor; Alumnae Achievement Award on the 50th anniversary of her graduation from Radcliffe College; a garden named in her honor at her Alma Mater, as well as a fountain named for her loyal teacher/companion, Anne Sullivan Macy; an entire room devoted to her, called the Helen Keller Room, at the American Foundation for the Blind in New York City and the establishment of her birthplace, "Ivy Green," in Tuscumbia, Alabama as a permanent shrine on 7 May 1954. Helen Keller also received honorary doctoral degrees from Harvard and Temple Universities, as well as the Universities of Glasgow, Scotland; Berlin, Germany; Delhi, India; and Witwatersrand in Johannesburg, South Africa. She was also an Honorary Fellow of the Educational Institute of Scotland.[357]

How does one measure greatness? Certainly one measure is that of not only overcoming immense adversity in one's life but also generating a wave of inspiration and hope for countless millions and leaving in that wake, a legacy of renown the world over. Helen Keller was such an individual, a paragon of icons and a legend history will not forget. In her tribute, the following poem is offered by William Ernest

King

Henley, himself a tribute to the indomitable human spirit in overcoming adversity.

Invictus

William Ernest Henley

Out of the night that covers me,
Black as the Pit from pole to pole,
I thank whatever gods may be
For my unconquerable soul.

In the fell clutch of circumstance
I have not winced nor cried aloud.
Under the bludgeonings of chance
My head is bloody, but unbowed.

Beyond this place of wrath and tears
Looms but the horror of the shade,
And, yet, the menace of the years
Finds, and shall find me, unafraid.

It matters not how strait the gate,
How charged with punishments the scroll,
I am the master of my fate;
I am the captain of my soul.

The Age of the Female II: Heroines of the Shift

Indira Gandhi

Statesman

You must learn to be still in the midst of activity
and to be vibrantly alive in repose. [358]

Indira Gandhi

By the end of the Twentieth Century, India maintained a population of one billion people; basically one-sixth of the world population. To put this number in perspective, imagine squeezing the entire population of the United States into the area east of the Mississippi River and multiplying it four times.[359] To this enormous number of people and the pressures it would naturally generate, include a plethora of upwards of two hundred separate and distinct national languages (not dialects) and 387 living languages, as well as five major religions: Hindu, Muslim, Christian, Buddhist and Sikh.[360] Next, try imagining being the leader of such a country. If that is not enough of a challenge, try being its first female Prime Minister. Feel the pressure and the challenge? An enormous task.

Such was the state of affairs inherited by Indira Gandhi, India's first female Prime Minister. Born on 19 November 1917 in Allahabad, India,[361] as Indira Priyadarshini Nehru, she was the only child of Jawaharlal Nehru, India's very first Prime Minister who took office on 15 August 1947 when India achieved sovereignty from Great Britain. Nehru served as India's leader until 1954, dying in 1964. His legacy would be extended through his daughter and her son. Indira Gandhi eventually became Prime Minister of India and was, undeniably, one of the most powerful and well-respected leaders of her time. Nehru's grandson, Rajiv Gandhi, Indira's second son, also became Prime Minister of India. Unfortunately, both Nehru's daughter and grandson were killed violently.[362]

To be clear, Indira Gandhi was not related to the famous Indian leader and political activist Mohatmas Gandhi. She came to her famous name by marriage. Her husband was Feroze Gandhi, a journalist, unrelated to Mohatmas Gandhi. Indira knew Feroze from childhood; they married in March of 1942.[363] He died in 1960.[364]

Gandhi followed in her famous father's (Nehru's) footsteps and was India's Prime Minister from 1966 to 1977; then again from 1980 to 1984, an extremely long reign for a leader of any democracy, especially one with such a complex and diverse society as that of India.[365]

As most political leaders, Indira Gandhi had her controversial moments during her tenure of political leadership. Her long political life saw her rise to power, be convicted and subsequently incarcerated for violating election laws, be exonerated by the Indian Supreme Court, spectacularly return to power, experience the death of one son, Sanjay, whom she was grooming to follow in her footsteps, manage a war between Pakistan and India which India won in 1971, deal with terrorist threats and uprisings, expand and encourage the study of information technology within her country, insure India's military strength through development of nuclear weaponry and be challenged by her country's economy, political corruption and poor standard of living. Through it all, notwithstanding her naysayers, Indira Gandhi was a woman of extraordinary political skills, endurance, tenacity and capability, exuding a tough and shrewd acumen. During her life she acquired a formidable international reputation as a statesman and political leader.[366]

Sadly and unfortunately, Indira Gandhi, like Mohatmas Gandhi, met with an assassin's bullet. Under her leadership, her government crushed a Sikh secessionist militant uprising led by Jarnail Singh Bindranwale in Amritsar, India, in June of 1984. During the operation, the Golden Temple of Amritsar, a holy Sikh shrine, was damaged. In retaliation, Indira Gandhi was shot to death by two of her own Sikh bodyguards in the garden of her official residence in New Delhi[367] on 31 October 1984. Her son, Rajiv, followed in her footsteps and served as Prime Minister of India until 1989. This made him the third member of his family to be Prime Minister of India, following, of course, in the footsteps of his grandfather, Jawaharlal Nehru and his mother, Indira Gandhi. Rajiv was killed in a bombing on 21 May 1991 at an election rally in Madras.[368]

Jacqueline Kennedy Onassis
First Lady of Ladies

*If you bungle raising your children,
I don't think whatever else you do well matters very much.*[369]
Jackie Kennedy Onassis

The assassination of President John Fitzgerald Kennedy (JFK) in Dallas, Texas, on 22 November 1963, was one of the most stultifying, paralyzing, painful, tearful, horrific, shocking, unbelievable and heart-wrenching events of Twentieth Century America. It was a surreal nightmare almost beyond explanation. From television commentators to soldiers, athletes, blue and white collar businessman, adults and children all across the country, the United States fell headlong into a state of stunned disbelief, agonizing lamentation and woeful sorrow.

However, throughout that horrific national experience, there was a quiet, controlled grace, refined dignity, superhuman strength and incredibly remarkable courage that helped quell the tidal wave of human emotion sweeping the country. That grace, that dignity, that strength and courage came in the presence of the survivor most heavily inflicted and afflicted with JFK's murder, the wife of the President himself, First Lady, Jacqueline Bouvier Kennedy.

Born Jacqueline Lee Bouvier on 28 July 1929 in Southampton, New York, Jackie Kennedy received her primary education from the best private schools. Beginning her collegiate career at Vassar, she graduated from George Washington University in 1952. Four years earlier in 1948, she had been dubbed "Debutante of the Year." In 1953 she married then United States Senator John F. Kennedy.[370]

When JFK was elected President in 1960, the fairy-tale reign of American Camelot began. John Kennedy was a handsome, charismatic, dynamic, youthful, President. His wife, Jacqueline, was a beautiful, equally charismatic, cultivated, dignified, intelligent, gracious, quiet, style-setting First Lady. In their own ways, each endeared themselves to the American public.

During JFK's short reign before being the youngest United States President ever assassinated in office, Jackie Kennedy redefined the role of First Lady. Her aristocratic and cultured upbringing, as well as her personal charm and grace, filled the White House with feminine refinement, elegance, intelligence, cultured taste, embraceable charm and loveliness. Defining her major role as that of taking care of the President, she devoted much of her time to making the White House a museum of American history and decorative arts. And, of course, the caring for her children, Caroline and John Jr., was a paramount focus. As she stated responsibly and lovingly: "If you bungle raising your children, I don't think whatever else you do well matters very much."[371]

Jacqueline Kennedy's gallant courage and strength in the aftermath of her husband's assassination undeniably won the admiration of the entire world. To have witnessed her grace under pressure, her controlled composure, her refined dignity during a time in which the world would have not even questioned forgiving or blaming her for 'losing it,' was a great inspiration of Twentieth Century America. It was her composed, collected consciousness of caring, not only for her husband, the President, but also for the Presidency of the United States in a time of tremendous tragedy and extreme personal adversity, that unquestionably helped keep the spirit of America together and indelibly elevated her to heroic heights, making her the First Lady of Ladies.

In 1968 Jacqueline Kennedy married wealthy Greek businessman, Aristotle Onassis, twenty-three years her senior. He died in March of 1975. From 1978 until her passing in 1994, Jacqueline Kennedy Onassis worked in New York as an editor for Doubleday Book Publishers.[372] Yet, her greatest role in life, and the one for which she will be most remembered, will be her exquisite elegance and grace in the face of the most painful of moments, both on a personal and national level. Without a doubt, Jacqueline Lee Bouvier Kennedy Onassis is one of the brightest stars in the night sky of the Twentieth Century.

King

Lucille Ball

Entertainer - Entrepreneur

The secret of staying young is to live honestly,
eat slowly, and lie about your age.

I'm not funny. What I am is brave. [373]
Lucille Ball

It is legion and legend - individuals being told they have absolutely no talent, skill or ability in their chosen field and then rising above the din of doubt to the clamoring currents and clarion call of adulation, admiration, applause and super stardom. Such was the history of one of the world's most beloved and successful entertainers, Lucille Ball.

Born on 6 August 1911 in Jamestown, New York, Lucille Ball was a mega matriarch in the entertainment business, both as a comedienne and an astute business woman. From an early age, her desire was to be an actress. With her mother's blessing, Ball left high school at age 15, went to New York and enrolled in the John Murray Anderson Drama School. Although she had many auditions, she was consistently told she had no talent and was not accepted to the school.[374]

Choosing to believe in herself more than her critics, Lucy pressed on. Using the name Diane Belmont, she took a job as a model and became an Earl Carrol showgirl. This led to a modeling position for Hattie Carnegie, a popular fashion designer of the day, who chose Ball to be the Chesterfield Cigarette Girl in 1933. At twenty-two years of age, Lucy received her first national exposure which would lead to a string of minor movie roles, the first of which was an appearance in Eddie Cantor's musical, "Roman Scandals."[375]

Lucy would not strike gold, at least not yet and not in the movie medium, even though she appeared in over 60 films by the late 1940s. Destiny, however, would not deny her talent, talent others told her repeatedly she did not have. After falling in love with the popular Cuban band leader, Desi Arnaz, the two were married in 1940. Together they developed the idea of a television show featuring the wacky marriage of a wild redhead and a Cuban band leader which they pitched to CBS and which CBS rejected. Not to be dissuaded, and believing in their own artistry, they formed a production company called "Desilu" and hit the American Road with a vaudeville act. They then used their money to film a pilot episode of their show, "I Love Lucy," which premiered in 1951. It was an instant success, so much so that CBS picked it up before the thirty minute episode was even over![376] Gold was struck. History was made.

"I Love Lucy" became the number one television show in the country and remained in that position for its first four years. In its entire first run history, "I Love Lucy" never fell below a number 3 Neilsen rating and received more than 200 awards and 5 Emmys. Even today it is syndicated in over 80 countries and has been viewed by billions of people.[377]

Life has its two sides, however, and its sadnesses. In 1960, Lucille Ball and Desi Arnaz divorced and went their separate ways. However, before their split Desilu Productions had become a powerful and respected corporation in the entertainment business, producing not just its own shows but such mega hits as Star Trek and Mission Impossible.

Seeing its value, Lucy took out a $3 million dollar loan and bought out her ex-husband's interest in Desilu, at the time the world's largest production facility. Obviously, Lucille Ball was not just a talented, ditzy comedienne but an extremely astute business woman and provider of jobs for many people. In 1967 she sold Desilu Productions for 17 million dollars, netting some $10 million.[378]

Lucille Ball history is still being made today. Somewhere in the world a show featuring Lucille Ball in "I Love Lucy," "The Lucy-Desi Comedy Hour," "The Lucy Show," "Here's Lucy" or "Life with Lucy" is being viewed on a television screen by some adoring fan. Talk about charisma, longevity and success!

Lucille Ball died from a ruptured aorta on 26 April 1989 when she was 77.[379] Her life and legacy are a reflection more of courage and bravery than talent, as she herself has stated: "I'm not funny. What I am is brave." Notice the affirmative self confidence and self awareness. She doesn't say "I don't' *think* I'm funny, I *think* I'm brave." She says, point blank: "I'm not funny. What I am is brave." Here's a woman who knew herself, who knew her abilities, who knew her potentialities and never let anyone else's opinion or criticism dissuade her from following her dreams - no ifs, ands or buts about it. So . . . so much for having no talent. So much for other people's opinions and criticisms. So much for believing in oneself. So much for courage and bravery. Way to go, Lucy! Thanks for the unforgettable memories . . . and the life lessons . . . and, most of all, for the inspiration!

Margaret Mead
Anthropologist

Never doubt that a small group of thoughtful,
committed citizens can change the world.
Indeed, it is the only thing that ever has.

We are living beyond our means. As a people
we have developed a life-style that is draining the earth
of its priceless and irreplaceable resources without regard
for the future of our children and people all around the world.

Women want mediocre men, and men are working
to become as mediocre as possible. [380]

Anthropology is the scientific study of the origin, the behavior and the physical, social, and cultural development of human beings. It has been stated that Margaret Mead, during the course of her 77 year old life (born: 16 December 1901; dying 15 November 1978),[381] was the most famous anthropologist in the entire world. It was through her work that the science of anthropology was introduced to many people around the globe.[382]

The child of a professor at the Wharton School of Finance at the University of Pennsylvania, Mead's early life was a transient one, living in New Jersey, New York and Pennsylvania.[383] She attended Barnard College, majoring in psychology and then earning her doctorate from Columbia University in anthropology.[384] She served as curator of ethnology at the American Museum of Natural History in New York

City, as well as being a full professor and head of the social science department at the Liberal Arts College of Fordham University.[385]

Margaret Mead was the first anthropologist to view human development in a cross-cultural perspective,[386] to study child-rearing practices and to conduct psychologically-oriented field work.[387] Mead also demonstrated that gender roles depend on culture as much as biology and differ from one society to another. She also studied the symbolic interweaving of child rearing and adults, affirmed that humans can learn from one another, that the diversity of human kind was a resource rather than a handicap, that the human capacity to change should be enhanced and supported, that cultural patterns of racism, warfare and environmental exploitation were learned, that societal traditions could be reconstructed and reorganized into new institutions,[388] that the ideal of family was extremely important and that children are critical to the survival of society because in them there is hope.[389]

Authoring some twenty books and co-authoring an equal number, Mead's work , translated into scores of languages, contributed greatly to the understanding of human history and impacted the daily lives of people worldwide.[390] Her insights into human kind were widely recognized. She received 28 honorary doctoral degrees, served as President of the American Anthropological Association and the American Association for the Advancement of Science and was posthumously awarded the Presidential Medal of Freedom.[391]

Books by Margaret Mead include: *Growing Up in New Guinea*; *The Changing Culture of an Indian Tribe*; *People and Places*; *Anthropology: A Human Science*; *An Anthropologist at Work: Writings* of Ruth Benedict; *Culture and Commitment*; *Rap on Race*,[392] *Coming of Age in Samoa* and *Growing Up in New Guinea*.[393]

Margaret Thatcher
Statesman

If you want to cut your own throat,
don't come to me for a bandage.

Pennies do not come from heaven.
They have to be earned here on earth.

Being powerful is like being a lady.
If you have to tell people you are, you aren't.

If you just set out to be liked, you would be
prepared to compromise on anything at any time,
and you would achieve nothing.

Disciplining yourself to do what you know is right
and important, although difficult, is the highroad to pride,
self-esteem, and personal satisfaction.

You may have to fight a battle more than once to win it.

I do not know anyone who has got to the top without hard work.
That is the recipe. It will not always get you to the top,
but should get you pretty near. [394]

King

Great leaders are great leaders because they lead, they go first and show the way. Not given to the indecisiveness of vacillation, leaders make tough choices and take tough stands; they come from a universal place of what is right, not what is popular, and they'd rather be hated for what they are than loved for what they are not. Great leaders stand alone. They have backbone . . . and grit. They also have keen minds, unyielding spirits and iron wills.

Margaret Thatcher, born Margaret Hilda Roberts[395] on 13 October 1925, was a true leader, the first female Prime Minister of England and the first British Prime Minister to serve three consecutive terms (1979 - 1990). Nicknamed 'The Iron Lady' by the Soviets, but being quite a lady in the truest sense of the word, Margaret Thatcher exuded an iron, formidable will. Her political philosophy, personal presence, pragmatic point of view and no nonsense sentiments generated an impact on the world of men and women that was both sweeping and enduring.[396]

If you want to cut your own throat, she said, don't come to me for a bandage, i.e., don't make other people responsible for your actions. *Pennies do not come from heaven. They have to be earned here on earth,* i.e., get working, not wishing. *Being powerful is like being a lady. If you have to tell people you are, you aren't,* i.e., actions speak louder than words. *If you just set out to be liked, you would be prepared to compromise on anything at any time, and you would achieve nothing,* i.e., leadership is not a popularity contest. These are just a sampling of Thatcher's thoughts, thoughts streaming from the well spring of solid character and individual self-worth within her.

Thatcher, whose father was a grocer, received a Master of Arts degree in Chemistry from Oxford and worked as a research chemist upon graduation.[397] Following a love of politics after becoming a tax lawyer, she joined England's Conservative Party and was elected to the House of Commons in 1959. From 1970 to 1974 she was Minister of Education and Science under Edward Heath and won the leadership of her party in 1975. In 1979 she led her party to victory and began her historic three term residency as Prime Minister of Great Britain.[398]

Thatcher, who believed in free markets and free minds, was a strong proponent of privatization, the transformation of business from governmental ownership to private control.[399] Under free market principles, *British Airways* was transformed from a sluggish national carrier to one of the best and most profitable airlines in the world. *British Steel*, which had lost more than a billion pounds during the final years of its state-owned identity, became the largest steel company in Europe. Privatization, a fundamental ideology of Thatcherism, caught on, and not just within British boundaries. By the end of the 1980s, not only had the term privatization caught on in Britain, more than 50 countries worldwide had created programs based on its concepts.[400]

As a leader, Thatcher clearly understood that politicians had to give clear orders to military leaders. Such decision-making acumen was evident in her decision to send British forces to the Falkland Islands in 1982 to defeat the Argentines who were claiming the Falklands as their own. The British victory was a great boon to the Thatcher administration and was a major cause for her landslide victory in 1983 for her second term.[401]

Thatcher's grit was evidenced in 1984. The IRA (Irish Republican Army), an organization dedicated to ending British rule in Northern Ireland, exploded a bomb at a Conservative Party conference in Brighton which nearly killed her and members of her government. In her tough and typical 'Iron Lady' style, Thatcher insisted the conference continue, in spite of this obvious assassination attempt.[402]

Margaret Thatcher's historic reign as Prime Minister of Great Britain came with her resignation in 1990 over differences on European Community policy. During that year she was awarded the Order of Merit in recognition of her extremely distinguished service.[403] In 1992 she entered the House of Lords (part of the United Kingdom Parliament) and in 1994 was entitled Baroness Thatcher of Kesteven.[404]

Margaret Thatcher was, indeed, a powerful figure of Twentieth Century earth. Her legacy will live on with her as being a feminine 'Iron Lady' of substance and stature, a champion of free minds and free markets who helped insure the continuance of a free world.

Marilyn Monroe
Cinematic Siren and Institution

It is a disease of our profession that we believe a woman with physical appeal has no talent. Marilyn is as near a genius as any actress I ever knew. She is an artist beyond artistry. She is the most completely realized and authentic film actress since Garbo. She has that same unfathomable mysteriousness. She is pure cinema.
- Joshua Logan - Director of Bus Stop[405]

Marilyn had the power. She was the wind, that comet shape that Blake draws blowing around a sacred figure. She was the light, and the goddess, and the moon; the

The Age of the Female II: Heroines of the Shift

space and the dream, the mystery and the danger, but
everything else all together, too, including Hollywood,
and the girl next door that every guy wants to marry.
Bert Stern - Author of The Last Sitting 406

[1] http://www.dsptech.demon.co.uk/marilyn/

...She gave more to the still camera than
any actress...any woman...I've ever photographed.
Richard Avedon [407]

Hollywood's a place where they'll pay you a thousand
dollars for a kiss, and fifty cents for your soul. [408]

My work is the only ground I've ever had to stand on.
I seem to have a whole superstructure with no
foundation--but I'm working on the foundation. [409]

I want to be a big star more than anything.
It's something precious.[410]

In the world of notoriety, some people become famous; some rise to super-stardom; others transcend their celebrity to become icons, but it is a rare few who become institutions. Marilyn Monroe was an institution.

Born Norma Jeane Mortenson on 1 June 1926 in Los Angeles, California, to Gladys Baker, a psychologically distressed mother who was later committed to a health care facility, Marilyn Monroe never knew her father and spent much of her youth in foster homes and orphanages. Norma Jeane received the surname Baker at her baptismal, but at age twenty in 1956, legally changed her name to Marilyn Monroe. 'Marilyn' was derived from the first name of stage actress Marilyn Miller and 'Monroe' from her mother's maiden name.[411]

Arguably, during the 20th Century Marilyn Monroe was the most famous star of the silver screen. She exuded a blend of vulnerability, innocence, glamour, and blond bombshell sexuality that hypnotized and captivated the modern world. She was basically discovered by a photographer named David Conover in 1944 while working in a factory inspecting parachutes to support the war effort.[412] In reflection of her inmost desires to be a big star, Monroe did not betray her dreams. She was a natural in front of the camera, and with a successful modeling career in ascendance, she landed a studio contract with 20th Century Fox on 26 August 1946, divorced her first husband, Jimmy Dougherty, whom she had married two years earlier, dyed her hair blonde, changed her name officially to Marilyn Monroe and, just like that, presto poof, a legend was born.[413] It's the stuff dreams and fairy tales are made of.

And a legend she was to become too. Of her thirty movies, the first was "The Shocking Miss Pilgrim" in 1947. She had a bit part and played bit parts until 1950 when she appeared in John Huston's thriller "The Asphalt Jungle." The same year she appeared in "All About Eve" which starred film great Bette Davis. It was Monroe's performance as Rose Loomis in "Niagara" in 1953 that delivered her to stardom. Following would come lead roles in "Gentlemen Prefer Blondes" which co-starred Jane Russell and "How to Marry a Millionaire" which featured film giants Lauren Bacall and Betty Grable. In 1953 at the age of 27, she was voted Best New Actress by Photoplay Magazine. She went on to star in other movies including "Bus Stop," "The Prince and the Showgirl" and "Some Like It Hot" for which she won a Golden Globe for Best Actress in a Comedy.[414]

Aside from being a famous actress, Monroe married famous baseball great Joe DiMaggio in 1954. Her second marriage, it unfortunately didn't even survive the first year. Her sexual image and their conflicting careers were major contributing factors to their split. Monroe and DiMaggio divorced on 27 October 1954, just nine months after they had wed. They did, however, remain friends.

It was not long before Monroe wedded a third time. On 29 June 1956 she married playwright Arthur Miller. He created the part of Roslyn Taber for her in the 1961 movie, "The Misfits." It was to be her last movie. Likewise, her marriage to Miller would also be her last. The couple divorced on 20 January 1961, four and a half years after their marriage nuptials. Although Monroe's success at long-term marriage was decidedly dismal, her personal magnetism and professional success were not. At the Golden Globes the following year (1962) she was named female World Film Favorite.[415]

Although living a famous public life of glitter and glamour, Monroe's personal life was steeped in pain, personal insecurity, instability, mystery and tragedy. Her own quotes give a sense of her personal battles and turmoils. Voluptuous and desirable, she was alleged to have had affairs with President of the United States John F. Kennedy, his brother Robert Kennedy, Attorney General of the United States, as well as with other famous men, among whom were Marlon Brando, Frank Sinatra and Elia Kazan.[416] Such lifestyle choices, spiritually speaking, could not have generated the wholeness and completeness necessary for the strong personal foundation needed for leading a strong, healthy and stable life. By her own statement: *My work is the only ground I've ever had to stand on. I seem to have a whole superstructure with no foundation--but I'm working on the foundation.* [417]

Was Marilyn Monroe, in essence, a little girl lost, a beautiful but fragile damsel in distress looking for the father she never had, the masculine love she never knew? Would her life have been more stable had she been raised by a devoted, nurturing, compassionate father? Perhaps. However, her destiny did not avail her of such a fate. Interestingly, her life was somewhat like that of Princess Diana of Wales who would follow her into a very similar destiny. Both were beautiful women in search of love; both had unhappy childhoods, fame beyond belief, multiple romantic heartaches, marriages to famous men, adoration from the multitudes, paparazzi pressure beyond compare, mysterious liaisons, tragic deaths, short lives and legacies of renown reserved only for incandescent heroines.

What is even more interesting is that, numerologically, their very public, luminous lives were extremely interwoven and, in many ways, mirrors. Both Marilyn Monroe and Princess Diana had 25/16/7 Lifepaths, 85/13/4 Expressions, 110/11-2 P/Es, 5 and 7 in their Challenges, 1-4-5 and 8 in their Pinnacles and 8 Voids. Both were also born on the 1st of the month (Marilyn on 1 June; Diana on 1 July), both died tragically in the month of August (the 8th calendar month: remember the 8 void in their charts?) at the age of 36 while in their 2nd Pinnacle/Challenge period under mysterious circumstances, and both had 19 letters in their natal names, creating an 8 challenge with a 1 theme! And this is the result of only a surface analysis. It is no wonder their fates were similar. The energies of their lives and destinies were strikingly interconnected; in many ways, identical. Identical energies produce identical results. It is the science of life. One plus One make Two, not Three. Thus, they were practically sisters, at least in the vibrational sense. From a fantasy viewpoint, and in retrospect of their lives lived, how interesting it would be to be a fly on the wall during their conversations (if their lives could have crossed paths) as they each recounted and shared their destinies with one another! It would, no doubt, mythologically, be the highest rated television show in history, notwithstanding the Babe Didrikson-Jackie Joyner Kersee Made-for-TV Special (again, another fantasy production).

Marilyn's famously fabled life ended like a Shakespearean tragedy. On 5 August 1962, her lifeless body was found at her home in Brentwood, California. She had apparently died in her sleep, victim of a drug overdose. But was the overdose intentionally self-inflicted, giving thought to the idea of suicide? Was it an accidental overdose? Was it inflicted by someone else? Was Marilyn Monroe, in fact, murdered? There is much speculation as to the latter, and controversy of such a homicide has not been quieted to this day. Still, her death is a mystery, much like the mystery involved in the assassination of JFK just 15 months later on 22 November 1963.[418]

There is no doubt Marilyn Monroe was bigger than life, the quintessential blonde whose gorgeous face, figure and siren-like seductive persona mesmerized the masses. She was more than a common star, more than a super-star. She was a goddess of film and fantasy, a veritable cinematic siren, whose fame and flame would forever light the halls and walls of 20th Century celebrity.

Still, however, Marilyn Monroe was a common soul and, like many of us, somewhat lost and sadly in need of the love and nurturing she never found. But when one thinks that she died just 12 years after the midpoint of the 20th Century (1962) and that her memory and magic still mesmerize people today, one is given to ponder the true power of personality that she possessed - this common, ordinary little girl with a dream to become a star, who transcended super-stardom and, in a relatively short professional life of sixteen years, became, not just a movie legend, but a veritable cinematic institution.

Oprah Winfrey
Media Queen

I always knew I was destined for greatness.

Think like a queen. A queen is not afraid to fail.
Failure is another steppingstone to greatness.[419]

If there has ever been a queen of the media, it is Oprah Winfrey. No woman in history has made more of an impact on so many lives through so many avenues of communication as she. The Oprah aura has exhibited itself through entrepreneurial enterprise, television, theater, film, music, radio and print media. Additionally, she has been heavily involved with education, philanthropy and humanitarian outreach. Her intuitions of personal greatness and royal reflections have, indeed, become manifest in her life, lifting her to the throne of a multi-media empire and a billion dollar fortune. Unquestionably and irrefutably, Oprah Winfrey is one of the most celebrated women of her time and, arguably, *the* most admired and beloved woman in America.

Born Oprah Gail Winfrey on 29 January 1954 on the family farm in Kosciusko, Mississippi, Oprah's early life was filled with the fires of adversity from the time she exited her mother's womb, fires that would fuel an ambition to achieve and serve others. Her parents (Vernon Winfrey and Vernita Lee) were young and unmarried and, in fact, they never married, and when her mother took a job in Milwaukee, Wisconsin shortly after her birth, Oprah's maternal grandmother, Hattie Mae Lee, cared for her, making sure the young Winfrey attended church, learned to read, recite poetry and Biblical verse.[420] As Oprah reminiscences:

> *I was taught to read at an early age. By the time I was three, I was reciting speeches in the church. They'd put me up on the program, and say, 'Little Mistress Winfrey will render a recitation,' and I would do 'Jesus rose on Easter Day, Hallelujah, Hallelujah, all the angels did proclaim.* [421]

There would, however, be no personal, positive 'hallelujahs' in her early years. Oprah was shuffled between grandmother, mother and father during her adolescence. As a young girl, and by her open confession, she had been molested and raped multiple times. Understandably, she was rebellious, unruly, wild. At fourteen she became pregnant and gave birth to a stillborn son. It was a devastation that turned her life around.[422]

Finally being sent to live with her father, Oprah received the discipline she needed. Vernon established strict rules, set curfews and demanded weekly book readings and reports. The enforced structure paid off. In 1972 she was named Nashville's Miss Fire Prevention and

Miss Black Tennessee. As a sophomore at Tennessee State University, she became the first African-American anchor at WTVF-TV in Nashville.[423] The fortunes of her life had definitely shifted. The 'hallelujahs' she recited as a child now had positive substance. Her rise to fame, fortune and throne had now begun. The Queen of Media was emerging from her cocoon.

Subsequent years were witness to a remarkable ascent of personal success and achievement. Along the way Oprah dethroned the then current King of Talk, Phil Donahue, becoming the national Queen of Talk, i.e. the talk show format.[424] *The Oprah Winfrey Show*, which entered national syndication in 1986 and which has a viewing audience of 21 million viewers in 105 countries worldwide, has remained the #1 talk show for 16 straight seasons and has won an astounding 35 Emmy Awards®, making it the highest rated and celebrated talk show in television history.[425]

Destiny would not restrict Oprah Winfrey's talents simply to the world of talk show hosting. Exuding an inherent sense of diversity, she made her acting debut in 1985 in *The Color Purple*, a Steven Spielberg production for which she received both Academy Award and Golden Globe nominations for her efforts. In 1998 she also had a starring role as "Sethe" in *Beloved*, the Pulitzer Prize-winning novel-made-movie by Toni Morrison, the first African-American Nobel Laureate (Literature 1993). She has also received plaudits for performances in ABC's television productions: *Before Women Had Wings, The Women of Brewster Place* and *There Are No Children Here*.[426]

Fully out of her cocoon, the queen flew; her kingdom grew. Reversing her name, she founded and is chairman of Harpo Incorporated, Harpo Productions, Inc., Harpo Studios, Inc., Harpo

Films, Inc., Harpo Video, Inc. and Harpo Print, LLC[427] - truly a vast media empire which the 2003 edition of *Forbes* Magazine corroborated by naming Oprah Winfrey as the first African-American woman to become a billionaire.[428] Manifestations of her enterprises include: *Oprah's Book Club; O, The Oprah Magazine; Oprah's Angel Network; The Oprah Winfrey Foundations* and *The Oprah Winfrey Leadership Academy for Girls.*[429]

Those who rule in any field of endeavor do not do so without skill, talent and substance. It is no less with Oprah Winfrey. Although possessive of riches, fame and name, she exudes an understanding of life reserved only for those who are revered. For example, she says: *Real integrity is doing the right thing, knowing that nobody's going to know whether you did it or not;* [430] *Where there is no struggle, there is no strength*; *My philosophy is that not only are you responsible for your life, but doing the best at this moment puts you in the best place for the next moment; The more you praise and celebrate your life, the more there is in life to celebrate; Turn your wounds into wisdom*; *We can't become what we need to be by remaining what we are; If you come to fame not understanding who you are, it will define who you are* and *Lots of people want to ride with you in the limo, but what you want is someone who will take the bus with you when the limo breaks down.* [431] All of these quotations are clearly indicative of the fact than Oprah Winfrey has substance, depth, understanding and a searing sensitivity that is only demonstrated by one who has been tried in the fires of life.

Oprah's honors and awards are plentifully plethoric. First, in recognition of her accomplishments, *Time* magazine named her as one of the most influential people of the 20th Century in 1998, the same year in which she received The National Academy of Television Arts &

Sciences' Lifetime Achievement Award. She has personally received seven Emmy Awards for Outstanding Talk Show Host, while her show has received nine Emmy Awards. Individual accomplishments were also recognized in 1996 with the George Foster Peabody Individual Achievement Award and the IRTS (International Radio and Television Society) Gold Medal Award. 1997 saw her recognized by *Newsweek* magazine as the Most Important Person in Books and Media, and *TV Guide* extolled her as Television Performer of the Year. The National Book Foundation's 50th Anniversary Gold Medal was awarded to her in 1999 for her influential contribution to reading and books, and in 2002 she was honored at the 54th Annual Prime-Time Emmy Awards with the first ever Bob Hope Humanitarian Award.[432]

Yet, with all this, more needs to be said. Oprah Winfrey's energies are perfectly coincidental and harmonious with those of the Twentieth Century and the 2nd Millennium -The Age of the Female. Like Princess Diana and Marilyn Monroe, Oprah maintains an 11/2 PE Performance/Experience in her numerology chart, thus giving her a role to play on the great life stage that focuses on the Yin, on females, others, relationships, support, caring, togetherness, partnership and cooperation. However, unlike Marilyn Monroe and Princess Diana, Oprah's Soul energy is also a 2, which means that in her deepest desires she is driven to help, to support, to care, to be interpersonally involved with others in relationship and partnership. As well as driving and motivating her, this 2 Soul energy strengthens and magnifies her 2 P/E, as well as making her extremely comfortable with the life role she is playing. Furthermore, her Material Soul is a 6, reinforcing her desires to be nurturing, tender, compassionate, artistic, motherly, familial and community oriented. No two numbers in tandem are more personally nurturing and loving than the 2 and 6. For Oprah, therefore, partnership, relationship, togetherness, support, compassion and nurturing dominate not only her outer life but her inner being.

With open arms and a nurturing heart, Oprah Winfrey embraces humanity to give, not to take; to be a leader who is a servant, not an overlord. Her life has been one of triumph over adversity and power over weakness. Without a doubt, she is more than just a Queen of Media. She is and will remain to be a beacon in the night, a warm and embracing light of feminine effulgence, a coruscating diamond among diamonds.

Sandra Day O'Connor
United States Supreme Court Justice

A moment of silence is not inherently religious.

Do the best you can in every task,
no matter how unimportant it may seem
at the time. No one learns more about a problem
than the person at the bottom.[433]

Despite the encouraging and wonderful gains and the
changes for women which have occurred in my
lifetime, there is still room to advance and to promote
correction of the remaining deficiencies and imbalances.[434]

Free societies remain free through an establishment of order. Order is based on the rule of law. Laws are made by human minds. Since the founding of the United States of America and the inception of the Judiciary Act of 1789 authorizing a United States Supreme Court - the capstone of the American judicial system whose first assemblage was on 1 February 1790 [435] - no female mind has been allowed within the purview of its prestigious and esteemed inner circle, to sit on its hallowed bench, and to influence laws of the land. That is not until the United States Senate unanimously confirmed the appointment of the first female justice to the Supreme Court of the United States, Sandra Day O'Connor, who took her oath of office on 26 September 1981, becoming the 102nd Supreme Court Justice in America. [436]

The importance of the greatest country in the free world promoting a female to become an associate justice of the highest court in the land cannot be overlooked or underestimated. For nearly 191 years of Supreme Court history, the rule of American law was solely and wholly based in the workings of the male mind and its Yang energies. With O'Connor's appointment, however, female energy was now infused into the judicial decision making process. Yin had arrived at the pinnacle of the American Judicial System and assumed a penultimate position, the ultimate being Chief Justice of the Supreme Court of the United States. Such appointment of a female to such an august body is poignantly striking, especially because it occurred in the Twentieth Century amid the oncoming energy flow of the 2nd Millennium, The Age of the Female.

Sandra Day was born on 26 March 1930, in El Paso, Texas, and grew up on the 198,000 acre Lazy B Ranch in southeastern Arizona. An isolated life, Day learned to be tough and independent. By eight years old she was riding with the ranch cowboys, mending fences, driving trucks and firing her own .22 caliber rifle. From age five onward, Sandra lived with her grandmother, Mamie Wilkey, in El Paso during school months and was deeply influenced by her grandmother's strong will and elevated expectations.

Day's collegiate days were spent at Stanford University where she graduated in 1950, Magna Cum Laude in economics. Continuing at Stanford, she received her law degree in 1952, graduating third in a class of 102 students, a prophetic number since she was the 102nd Supreme Court Justice. That same year she married fellow law student, John Jay O'Connor III.

Finding it difficult to gain employment in the private sector as a female attorney, O'Connor accepted a deputy county attorney position in San Mateo, California, a job which corroborated her enjoyment of public office. After a hiatus as a full-time mother and doing volunteer work in multiple capacities from 1960 to 1965, O'Connor resumed regular employment as an assistant state attorney general. In 1969, Governor Jack Williams appointed her to the Arizona Senate upon evacuation of a position held by Isabel A. Burgess who accepted an appointment in Washington, D.C.. In 1972 she was elected majority leader, the first woman to hold such an office anywhere in America. O'Connor was elected to a state judgeship in 1974 and was appointed to the Arizona Court of Appeals in 1979. In 1981, President Ronald Reagan nominated O'Connor to the Supreme Court Justice seat vacated by Potter Steward, this in fulfillment of a campaign promise to appoint a woman to the Supreme Court.[437]

Thus, with the appointment of Sandra Day O'Connor as the first female and 102nd Supreme Court Justice of the United States, another

King

chapter of the rise of women in the annals of American history was made. It was also a move greatly important to the United States because freedom and "Equal Justice Under Law" - the inscription engraved on the very walls of the Supreme Court building and those qualities which America holds most dear - had been embraced, at least to a limited degree. Yang and Yin energies now established law in the greatest free country in the world and in the highest and most hallowed judicial halls of that country, although not in equal measure. It was, however and of course, a great step forward for female progress. The next major step in the ascendance of the Yin will be when a woman is either appointed as Chief Justice of the United States or elected to the American Presidency - events most probably destined to occur during this 2nd Millennium where the energy focus definitely highlights and showcases the female and her feminine attributes.

In conclusion, when Sandra Day O'Connor was asked in her Senate confirmation hearings as to what she would like her tombstone to say, she responded: "Here lies a good judge."[438] In all respect for her humility, for the sake of American history and in deference to her personal legacy, perhaps a more appropriate, accurate and inspirational tombstone inscription would be: "Here lies Sandra Day O'Connor, the First Female Supreme Court Justice of the United States of America."

CHAPTER FIVE

YIN SPEAK

'Tis words that move the pen
to subjugate the sword;
'Tis words that move men's hearts
where none can be ignored;
'Tis words that one remembers
within the dark of night
that lift the waning spirit
to wax within the light.
Words, words, words -
the lifeblood of the pen.
Hearken, man, and take to heart
these messages from the Yin.

Beneath the rule of men entirely great, the pen is mightier than the sword. So wrote 19th Century English novelist and playwright Edward George Earle Bulwer-Lytton in his play *Richelieu* (Act II Scene 3). And so it is. But is the mightiness of the pen obviated by great men or women? Is it not used by them as well? A sword can scar and kill the body, but cannot words scar the heart and kill the spirit? Can they not antithetically heal the heart and lift the spirit? What power truly rests within a sword? What power truly rests within a word? Who is there among us who has not been devastated, perhaps for

King

an entire lifetime, by a single, reckless word? Who is there also among us who has not been inspired to great heights or healing by a kind and gentle utterance?

To be sure, words are power. If words were flaccid and powerless, there would be no *Magna Charta*, no *Declaration of Independence*, no *Bill of Rights* or *Gettysburg Address*. There would be no wars, marches for peace, demonstrations or remonstrations. The actions taken by men upon hearing the words of great leaders would never have been. Had it not been for words, preachers would never have preached, teachers would never have taught, singers would never have sung, hearts would never have soared or fallen. Words are the strings of the heart and the vehicles of the mind. When plucked or strummed or banged in whatever manner or mean, they generate feelings from fear to elation. They also carry our thoughts along the highways and byways of the social spectrum. Words carry life. They also carry death . . . and laughter . . . and sadness . . . and joy . . . and sorrow. Words are, indeed, power. Following are some selected and exclusive words from over 200 women to inspire you, give you cause to ponder, cry, sigh, laugh, sing and smile as they relay the power of their own priceless and precious presence.

Words from Women: Quotes from the Yin

Abigail Adams

[Wife of John Adams, the second President of the United States of America]

Learning is not attained by chance, it must be sought for with ardor and attended to with diligence.

We have too many high sounding words, and too few actions that correspond with them.

Abigail Kelley Foster

[American abolitionist, radical social reformer and advocate of women rights]

Go where you are least wanted, for there you are most needed.

Abigail Van Buren (Dear Abby)

[Advice columnist of the mid-20th Century]

Wisdom doesn't automatically come with old age. Nothing does - except wrinkles. It's true, some wines improve with age. But only if the grapes were good in the first place.

Adelle Davis

[Pioneer American nutritionist of the mid-20th Century]

We are indeed much more than what we eat, but what we eat can nevertheless help us to be much more than what we are.

As I see it every day you do one of two things: build health or produce disease in yourself.

King

Adrienne E. Gusoff

[Freelance writer, lecturer, humorist, advice columnist and motivational speaker]

Girls just want to have funds.

Not only is life a bitch, it has puppies.

Agatha Christie

[19th Century English author, novelist, crime writer and playwright.]

One is left with the horrible feeling now that war settles nothing; that to win a war is as disastrous as to lose one.

Agnes DeMille

[20th Century American dancer and choreographer]

No trumpets sound when the important decisions of our life are made. Destiny is made known silently.

Agnes Repplier

[19th/20th Century American essayist]

There are few nudities so objectionable as the naked truth.

Alberta Lee Cox

[20th Century American women's basketball coach and horsewoman]

It's not enough to be good if you have the ability to be better. It is not enough to be very good if you have the ability to be very great.

Alice Roosevelt Longworth

[Eldest child of U.S. President Theodore Roosevelt]

If you can't say anything good about someone, sit right here by me.

Alice Walker

[20th Century American author and feminist]

Anybody can observe the Sabbath, but making it holy surely takes the rest of the week.

Althea Gibson

[1st African-American tennis player of global renown]

I always wanted to be somebody. If I made it, it's half because I was game enough to take a lot of punishment along the way and half because there were a lot of people who cared enough to help me. No matter what accomplishments you make, somebody helped you.

In sports, you simply aren't considered a real champion until you have defended your title successfully. Winning it once can be a fluke; winning it twice proves you are the best.

Amanda Cross

[Penname of Carolyn Gold Heilbrun, 20th Century American author and feminist]

The point of quotations is that one can use another's words to be insulting.

Amelia Burr

[19th/20th Century American poet]

Because I have loved life, I shall have no sorrow to die.

King

Amelia Earhart

[20th Century
American pioneer
aviatrix and author.
The first female to
fly across the
Atlantic Ocean solo
and the first person
to fly solo across the
Pacific Ocean]

Courage is the price that life exacts for granting peace.

Never interrupt someone doing what you said couldn't be done.

In soloing — as in other activities — it is far easier to start something than it is to finish it.

Flying may not be all plain sailing, but the fun of it is worth the price.

The most effective way to do it, is to do it. The more one does and sees and feels, the more one is able to do, and the more genuine may be one's appreciation of fundamental things like home, and love, and understanding companionship.

Never do things others can do and will do if there are things others cannot do or will not do.

Better do a good deed near at home than go far away to burn incense.
The greatest work that kindness does to others is that it makes them kind themselves.

The Age of the Female II: Heroines of the Shift

Amy Dacyczyn

[Author of *The
Tightwad Gazette*
and frugality expert]

Frugality without creativity is deprivation.

Amy Vanderbilt

[20th Century
American author on
etiquette]

The modern rule is that every woman
should be her own chaperon.

Anais Nin

[20th Century
Catalan-Cuban-
French author and
journalist]

Dreams are necessary to life.

When you make a world tolerable for
yourself, you make a world tolerable for
others.

Life shrinks or expands in proportion to
one's courage.

The personal life deeply lived always
expands into truths beyond itself.

I postpone death by living, by suffering,
by error, by risking, by giving, by losing.

Ann Landers

[20th Century
American advice
columnist]

Opportunities are usually disguised as
hard work, so most people don't recognize
them.

Anna Freud

[Psychoanalyst and
last daughter of
Sigmund Freud]

Creative minds have always been known
to survive any kind of bad training.

King

Anna Pavlova

[19th/20th Century
famed Russian
classical ballerina]

To follow, without halt, one aim: there's
the secret of success.

Anna Quindlen

[20th Century
American author,
journalist and
columnist]

If your success is not on your own terms,
if it looks good to the world but does not
feel good in your heart, it is not success at
all.

Anne Bradstreet

[17th Century
English/American
writer and poet;
Puritan emigrant]

If we had no winter, the spring would not
be so pleasant: if we did not sometimes
taste of adversity, prosperity would not be
so welcome.

Anne Frank

[Famous teenage
Jewish author of *The
Diary of Anne
Frank*; died in WWII
Nazi concentration
camp of Bergen-
Belsen]

Think of all the beauty still left around
you and be happy.
Whoever is happy will make others happy
too.

He who has courage and faith will never
perish in misery!

Anne Sullivan

[Famous tutor of
Helen Keller]

I have thought about it a great deal, and
the more I think, the more certain I am
that obedience is the gateway through
which knowledge, yes, and love, too, enter
the mind of the child.

The Age of the Female II: Heroines of the Shift

It is a rare privilege to watch the birth,
growth, and first feeble struggles of a
living mind.

People seldom see the halting and painful
steps by which the most insignificant
success is achieved.

Anne Tyler

[1989 Pulitzer Prize-
winning American
novelist]

People always call it luck when you've
acted more sensibly than they have.

Anne Wilson

Schaef

[20th Century author
on life and well-
being]

We begin to see that the completion of an
important project has every right to be
dignified by a natural grieving process.
Something that required the best of you
has ended. You will miss it.

Anne-Sophie

Swetchine

[18th/19th Century
Russian salon
hostess/philosopher]

Providence has hidden a charm in difficult
undertakings which is appreciated only by
those who dare to grapple with them.

Aung San Suu Kyi

[Burmese Nobel
Peace Prize
Laureate, 1991,
democracy advocate,
Prime Minister-elect;
imprisoned by
Burmese military
dictatorship]

The greatest gift for an individual or a
nation ...was abhaya, fearlessness, not
merely bodily courage but absence of fear
from the mind....Fearlessness may be a
gift, but perhaps more precious is the
courage acquired through endeavour,

Aung San Suu Kyi

courage that comes from cultivating the habit of refusing to let fear dictate one's actions, courage that could be described as grace under pressure -- grace which is renewed repeatedly in the face of harsh, unremitting pressure.

Ayn Rand

[20th Century Russian-American novelist, playwright, screenwriter and philosopher]

A creative man is motivated by the desire to achieve, not by the desire to beat others.

God... a being whose only definition is that he is beyond man's power to conceive.

Happiness is that state of consciousness which proceeds from the achievement of one's values.

Babe Didrikson

[20th Century American athlete and Olympic champion known for her great versatility in basketball, golf, track and field]

Before I was ever in my teens, I knew exactly what I wanted to be when I grew up. My goal was to be the greatest athlete that ever lived.

Luck? Sure. But only after long practice and only with the ability to think under pressure.

Winning has always meant much to me, but winning friends has meant the most.

The formula for success is simple: practice and concentration, then more practice and more concentration.

Barbara Bush

[First Lady of the United States (1989-1993), wife of the 41st President, George H.W. Bush and mother to George W. Bush, 43rd President of the U.S]

War is not nice.

Barbara Hall

[Canadian lawyer, politician and public servant]

You're alive. Do something.

Barbara Streisand

[American actress, singer, political activist, film producer and director]

The audience is the best judge of anything. They cannot be lied to. Truth brings them closer. A moment that lags - they're gonna cough.

Myths are a waste of time. They prevent progression.

Barbara Walters

[American writer, journalist, interviewer, newscaster, television hostess and media icon]

One may walk over the highest mountain one step at a time.

The world may be full of fourth-rate writers, but it's also full of fourth-rate readers.

King

Barbara Walters

Wait for those unguarded moments. Relax the mood and, like the child dropping off to sleep, the subject often reveals his truest self.

I was the kind nobody thought could make it. I had a funny Boston accent. I couldn't pronounce my R's. I wasn't a beauty.

Baroness Bertha von Suttner

[Austrian novelist, pacifist and the first woman to be a Nobel Peace Prize Laureate, 1905]

The question of whether violence or law shall prevail between states is the most vital of the problems of our eventful era. Inconceivable would be the consequence of the threatening world war which many misguided people are prepared to precipitate.

Bette Davis

[American actress of stage, television and film]

This became a credo of mine...attempt the impossible in order to improve your work.

There are new words now that excuse everybody. Give me the good old days of heroes and villains, the people you can bravo or hiss. There was a truth to them that all the slick credulity of today cannot touch.

Men become much more attractive when they start looking older. But it doesn't do much for women, though we do have an advantage: make-up.

Bette Midler

[American singer, actress and comedienne]

I never know how much of what I say is true.

Betty Friedan

[20th Century American writer, activist and feminist]

Men are not the enemy, but the fellow victims. The real enemy is women's denigration of themselves.

Betty Williams-Perkins

[Co-recipient of the Nobel Peace Prize, 1976, with Mairead Corrigan]

The Lord didn't start the wars or create the weapons, we did. From the slingshot on down, mankind has never created a weapon he didn't use.

Billy Jean King

[American tennis player, icon and promoter]

Champions keep playing until they get it right.

Be bold. If you're going to make an error, make a doozy, and don't be afraid to hit the ball.

I think self-awareness is probably the most important thing towards being a champion.

King

208

Bonnie Blair [American Gold Medal Speedskater]	I'm definitely going to miss hearing the sound of that gun.
Bonnie Friedman [Author and writer]	An unhurried sense of time is in itself a form of wealth.
Carolyn Wells [American author and poet]	Actions lie louder than words.
Carrie Fisher [American actress, screenwriter and novelist]	You can't find any true closeness in Hollywood, because everybody does the fake closeness so well.

Instant gratification takes too long. |
| Charlotte Bronte [Eldest of the three Bronte sisters, all of whom were famous British authors] | A ruffled mind makes a restless pillow.

Cheerfulness, it would appear, is a matter which depends fully as much on the state of things within, as on the state of things without and around us.

Neither birth nor sex forms a limit to genius. |
| Charlotte Perkins Gilman [American writer and feminist] | The first duty of a human being is to assume the right relationship to society-- more briefly, to find your real job, and do it. |

Charlotte Whitton

[Canadian mayor and feminist]

Whatever woman do they must do twice as well as men to be thought half as good. Luckily, this is not difficult.

Cher Bono

[American singer, actress, director and record producer]

Women have to harness their power - its absolutely true. It's just learning not to take the first no. And if you can't go straight ahead, you go around the corner.

Women are the real architects of society.

Cherrie Moraga

[Playwright, poet, essayist, teacher and lecturer]

When you are not physically starving, you have the luxury to realize psychic and emotional starvation.

Christa McAuliffe

I touch the future. I teach.

[First American teacher/astronaut in space, killed in the Challenger shuttle disaster of 28 January 1986]

What are we doing here? We're reaching for the stars.

I have a box of papers at home of [my own press coverage]. When I'm sixty, maybe, I'll look at my pile of papers and wonder, 'What really happened that year?'

Christina Baldwin

[American author and Co-founder of PeerSpirit]

Change is the constant, the signal for rebirth, the egg of the phoenix.

Christina Rossetti

[19th Century
English poet]

Silence is more musical than any song.

Christine Bovee

[Quotable author]

Doubt whom you will, but never yourself.

Clare Booth Luce

[American
playwright, editor,
journalist,
Ambassador to Italy
and Congressional
Representative]

Censorship, like charity, should begin at home; but, unlike charity, it should end there.

No good deed goes unpunished.

Courage is the ladder on which all the other virtues mount.

Love is a verb.

Corazon Aquino

[The 11th and first
female President of
the Philippines,
1986]

Reconciliation should be accompanied by justice, otherwise it will not last. While we all hope for peace it shouldn't be peace at any cost but peace based on principle, on justice.

Corra Harris

[19th/20th Century
American writer and
novelist]

The bravest thing you can do when you are not brave is profess courage and act accordingly.

Coretta Scott King

It doesn't matter how strong your opinions

[American activist, author and widow of Martin Luther King, Jr.]

are. If you don't use your power for positive change, you are, indeed, part of the problem.

Dianne Feinstein

[American Senator and first Mayor of San Francisco]

Toughness doesn't have to come in a pinstriped suit.

Dodie Smith

[English novelist and playwright]

Noble deeds and hot baths are the best cures for depression.

Dolly Parton

[American singer, songwriter, actress and author]

Leave something good in every day.

Dolores Huerta

[Chicana labor leader, co-founder and First Vice President Emeritus of the United Farm Workers of America]

If you haven't forgiven yourself something, how can you forgive others?

Dorothea Brande

[American writer and editor]

Act as if it were impossible to fail.

Dorothea Dix

[19th Century social activist]

I think even lying on my bed I can still do something.

Dorothy L. Sayers

[British author, poet, novelist, playwright]

A human being must have occupation if he or she is not to become a nuisance to the world.

Dorothy Nevill

[19th/20th Century British writer, hostess, horticulturalist]

The real art of conversation is not only to say the right thing at the right place but to leave unsaid the wrong thing at the tempting moment.

Dorothy Sarnoff

[American opera singer and actress]

Make sure you have finished speaking before your audience has finished listening.

Dr. Joyce Brothers

[American psychologist, writer, actress and advice columnist]

No matter how much pressure you feel at work, if you could find ways to relax for at least five minutes every hour, you'd be more productive.

Dr. Laura Schlessinger

[American psychologist, author, and radio host]

Don't spend time beating on a wall, hoping to transform it into a door.

Edith Nesbitt

[19th/20th Century British author, poet and dramatist]

It is wonderful how quickly you get used to things, even the most astonishing.

Edith Sitwell

[19th/20th Century British poet]

The public will believe anything so long as it is not founded on truth.

Edna Ferber

[19th/20th Century American playwright and novelist]

Perhaps too much of everything is as bad as too little.

Edna St. Vincent Millay

[19th/20th Century American poet and playwright; first woman to win Pulitzer Prize for poetry, 1923]

It's not true that life is one damn thing after another; it is one damn thing over and over.

Please give me some good advice in your next letter. I promise not to follow it.

Where you used to be, there is a hole in the world which I find myself constantly walking around in the daytime, and falling into at night. I miss you like hell.

Eleanor Roosevelt

[First Lady of the United States from 1933 to 1945; wife of U.S. President Franklin Delano Roosevelt (#32); diplomat, author, international activist, speaker]

What is to give light must endure the burning.

Only a man's character is the real criterion of worth.

Do what you feel in your heart to be right - for you'll be criticized anyway. You'll be damned if you do, and damned if you don't.

Eleanor Roosevelt

It is not fair to ask of others what you are unwilling to do yourself.

No one can make you feel inferior without your consent.

When you cease to make a contribution, you begin to die.

Justice cannot be for one side alone, but must be for both.

We are afraid to care too much, for fear that the other person does not care at all.

It isn't enough to talk about peace. One must believe in it. And it isn't enough to believe in it. One must work at it.

You gain strength, courage and confidence by every experience in which you really stop to look fear in the face. You are able to say to yourself, 'I have lived through this horror. I can take the next thing that comes along.' You must do the thing you think you cannot do.

A woman is like a tea bag- you never know how strong she is until she gets in hot water.

The Age of the Female II: Heroines of the Shift

I could not at any age be content to take my place in a corner by the fireside and simply look on.

I think that somehow, we learn who we really are and then live with that decision.

Life was meant to be lived, and curiosity must be kept alive.

One must never, for whatever reason, turn his back on life.

One thing life has taught me: if you are interested, you never have to look for new interests. They come to you. When you are genuinely interested in one thing, it will always lead to something else.

People grow through experience if they meet life honestly and courageously. This is how character is built.

You have to accept whatever comes and the only important thing is that you meet it with the best you have to give.

No matter how plain a woman may be, if truth and loyalty are stamped upon her face, all will be attracted to her.

King

Elisabeth Kubler-Ross

[20th Century Swiss-born psychiatrist famous for her teachings on death and dying]

Learn to get in touch with the silence within yourself and know that everything in this life has a purpose.

Elizabeth Barrett Browning

[19th Century British Victorian poet]

Measure not the work until the day's out and the labor done.

An ignorance of means may minister to greatness, but an ignorance of aims make it impossible to be great at all.

God's gifts put man's best dreams to shame.

Light tomorrow with today!

Since when was genius found respectable?

My sun sets to raise again.

Elizabeth Cady Stanton

[19th Century social activist and leader of the women's suffrage movement]

Self-development is a higher duty than self-sacrifice.

Truth is the only safe ground to stand on.

So long as women are slaves, men will be knaves.

Womanhood is the great fact in her life; wifehood and motherhood are but incidental relations.

It requires philosophy and heroism to rise above the opinion of the wise men of all nations and races.

Whatever the theories may be of woman's dependence on man, in the supreme moments of her life he can not bear her burdens.

Elizabeth Clarkson Zwart
[quotable author]

The older I grow, the less important the comma becomes. Let the reader catch his own breath.

Elizabeth Forsythe Hailey
[20th Century American playwright and journalist]

Time is a cruel thief to rob us of our former selves. We lose as much to life as we do to death.

Elizabeth Janeway
[20th Century American author]

We don't get offered crises, they arrive.

Elizabeth Taylor
[Famous American actress]

Success is a great deodorant. It takes away all your past smells.

If someone's dumb enough to offer me a million dollars to make a picture, I'm certainly not dumb enough to turn it down.

Ella Fitzgerald

[American jazz vocalist known as the First Lady of Song]

Just don't give up trying to do what you really want to do. Where there is love and inspiration, I don't think you can go wrong.

Ellen Metcalf

[quotable author]

You have to recognize when the right place and the right time fuse and take advantage of that opportunity. There are plenty of opportunities out there. You can't sit back and wait.

Elsa Maxwell

[19th/20th Century American author, songwriter and gossip columnist]

Laugh at yourself first before anyone else can.

Emily Greene Balch

[American writer, editor, academic, and pacifist; co-recipient of Nobel Peace Prize, 1946, with John Mott]

We have a long way to go. So let us hasten along the road, the road of human tenderness and generosity. Groping, we may find one another's hands in the dark.

Emily Dickinson

[19th Century poet]

Success is counted sweetest by those who ne'er succeed.

The Age of the Female II: Heroines of the Shift

To comprehend a nectar - Requires sorest
need.

It is better to be the hammer than the
anvil.

People need hard times and oppression to
develop psychic muscles.

Remember if you marry for beauty, thou
bindest thyself all thy life for that which
perchance, will neither last nor please thee
one year: and when thou hast it, it will be
to thee of no price at all.
Luck is not chance, it's toil; fortune's
expensive smile is earned.

Emma Goldman

[19th/20th Century
Lithuanian born U.S.
emigrant, political
activist and
anarchist]

The free expression of the hopes and
aspirations of a people is the greatest and
only safety in a sane society.

Erica Jong

[20th Century
American author and
teacher]

Advice is what we ask for when we
already know the answer but wish we
didn't.

Men and women, women and men. It will
never work.

King

Erica Jong

Take your life in your own hands and what happens? A terrible thing: no one to blame.

And the trouble is, if you don't risk anything, you risk even more.

Eva Bowring

[American U.S. Senator, 1954]

I'm going to have to ride the fence awhile until I find where the gates are.

Eve Babitz

[American author]

By the time I'd grown up, I naturally supposed that I'd be grown up.

Florence Griffith

Joyner: Flo-Jo

[American track and field athlete and Olympic Gold medalist plagued by allegations of steroid use]

I pray hard, work hard and leave the rest to God.

Florence

Nightingale

[19th Century British nurse, writer, statistician and advocate of medical care and sanitary hospital living conditions]

I can stand out the war with any man.

You ask me why I do not write something....I think one's feelings waste themselves in words, they ought all to be distilled into actions and into actions which bring results.

Women never have a half-hour in all their lives (excepting before or after anybody is up in the house) that they can call their own, without fear of offending or of hurting someone.

Why do people sit up so late, or, more rarely, get up so early? Not because the day is not long enough, but because they have 'no time in the day to themselves.'

It may seem a strange principle to enunciate as the very first requirement in a Hospital that it should do the sick no harm.

Frances Lear

[activist, magazine publisher and writer; wife of television producer Norman Lear]

Many older women are inhibited and afraid to act. It is such a waste of human potential.

Gail Godwin

[American novelist and short story writer]

Good teaching is one-fourth preparation and three-fourths theater.

George Eliot

[19th Century British novelist]

Be courteous, be obliging, but don't give yourself over to be melted down for the benefit of the tallow trade.

King

George Eliot

Blessed is the man who, having nothing to say, abstains from giving wordy evidence of the fact.

One must be poor to know the luxury of giving.

The golden moments in the stream of life rush past us and we see nothing but sand; the angels come to visit us, and we only know them when they are gone.

There's folks 'ud stand on their heads and then say the fault was i' their boots.

Animals are such agreeable friends - they ask no questions, they pass no criticisms.

The scornful nostril and the high head gather not the odors that lie on the track of truth.

It is vain to say human beings ought to be satisfied with tranquility: they must have action; and they will make it if they cannot find it.

Geraldine Ferraro

[American attorney, politician, congress

Modern life is confusing - no Ms take about it.

The Age of the Female II: Heroines of the Shift

woman and first woman Vice-Presidential candidate of a major political party (Democratic)]

It was not so very long ago that people thought that semiconductors were part-time orchestra leaders and microchips were very, very small snack foods.

Gloria Borger

[American political analyst, journalist, columnist, editor]

For most folks, no news is good news; for the press, good news is not news.

Gloria Vanderbilt

[American clothes designer, artist, actress and heiress]

That is the best - to laugh with someone because you both think the same things are funny.

Golda Meir

[Fourth Prime Minister of Israel, 1969 to 1974; referred to as the "Iron Lady of Israeli Politics"]

I must govern the clock, not be governed by it.

Those who don't know how to weep with their whole heart, don't know how to laugh either.

I can honestly say that I was never affected by the question of the success of an undertaking. If I felt it was the right thing to do, I was for it regardless of the possible outcome.

Whether women are better than men I cannot say - but I can say they are certainly no worse.

King

Golda Meir

Trust yourself. Create the kind of self that you will be happy to live with all your life. Make the most of yourself by fanning the tiny, inner sparks of possibility into flames of achievement.

To be successful, a woman has to be much better at her job than a man.

Old age is like a plane flying through a storm. Once you're aboard, there's nothing you can do.

There can be no doubt that the average man blames much more than he praises. His instinct is to blame. If he is satisfied he says nothing; if he is not, he most illogically kicks up a row.

Grace Kelly

[American film actress and Princess of Monaco]

The freedom of the press works in such a way that there is not much freedom from it.

Gracie Allen

[American comedienne; comic sidekick of husband George Burns]

When I was born I was so surprised I didn't talk for a year and a half.

Gwendolyn
Brooks
[American poet and
Library of Congress
Consultant in
Poetry]

We are each other's harvest; we are each other's business; we are each other's magnitude and bond.

Hannah Arendt
[20th Century
German-Jewish
political theorist]

Forgiveness is the key to action and freedom.

Harriet Lerner
[American clinical
psychologist]

Anger is a signal, and one worth listening to.

Harriet Martineau
[19th Century
British writer,
economist,
journalist, feminist]

Readers are plentiful; thinkers are rare.

Helen Gurley
Brown
[American author,
publisher and editor-
in-chief of
Cosmopolitan
magazine]

Money, if it does not bring you happiness, will at least help you be miserable in comfort.

Helen Hayes
[Actress; First Lady
of the American
Theater]

Always aim for achievement and forget about success.

Helen Keller

[American and
world-renowned
deaf/blind author,
lecturer and activist]

The best and most beautiful things in the world cannot be seen, nor touched . . . but are felt in the heart.

Although the world is full of suffering, it is full also of the overcoming of it.

Many persons have a wrong idea of what constitutes true happiness. It is not attained through self-gratification but through fidelity to a worthy purpose.

One can never consent to creep when one feels an impulse to soar.

We could never learn to be brave and patient if there were only joy in the world.

The highest result of education is tolerance.

Character cannot be developed in ease and quiet. Only through experience of trial and suffering can the soul be strengthened, ambition inspired, and success achieved.

I am only one; but still I am one. I cannot do everything, but still I can do something. I will not refuse to do something I can do.

Science may have found a cure for most evils; but it has found no remedy for the worst of them all--the apathy of human beings.

Indira Gandhi

[India's first female Prime Minister who served a total of fifteen years in multiple terms. She was assassinated by her own body guards on 31 October 1984]

The power to question is the basis of all human progress.

People tend to forget their duties but remember their rights.

You can't shake hands with a clenched fist.

Anger is never without an argument, but seldom with a good one.
We must learn to be still in the midst of activity and to be vibrantly alive in repose.

Irene Kassorla

[International psychologist, author and lecturer]

Don't wait for your ship to come in and feel angry and cheated when it doesn't. Get going with something small.

Irene Peter

[Author/essayist]

Ignorance is no excuse--it's the real thing.

Isabel Colegate

[British author and literary agent]

It is not a bad idea to get in the habit of writing down one's thoughts. It saves one having to bother anyone else with them.

228

Jackie Joyner Kersee

[American Olympic champion and one of the greatest female athletes of all time]

Once I leave this earth, I know I've done something that will continue to help others.

I think it's the mark of a great player to be confident in tough situations.

The medals don't mean anything and the glory doesn't last. It's all about your happiness. The rewards are going to come, but my happiness is just loving the sport and having fun performing.

Jacqueline Kennedy Onassis

[First Lady and wife of the 35th President of the United States, John F. Kennedy; editor for Doubleday publishing company]

There are two kinds of women: those who want power in the world, and those who want power in bed.

An Editor becomes kind of your mother. You expect love and encouragement from an Editor.

When Harvard men say they have graduated from Radcliffe, then we've made it.

If you bungle raising your children, I don't think whatever else you do matters very much.

The Age of the Female II: Heroines of the Shift

Can anyone understand how it is to have
lived in the White House and then,
suddenly, to be living alone as the
President's widow?

Jan Ashford

[quotable author]

There is no such thing as can't, only won't.
If you're qualified, all it takes is a burning
desire to accomplish, to make a change.
Go forward, go backward. Whatever it
takes! But you can't blame other people or
society in general. It all comes from your
mind. When we do the impossible we
realize we are special people.

Jane Addams

[Social activist and
Nobel Peace
Laureate, 1931]

I do not believe that women are better than
men. We have not wrecked railroads, nor
corrupted legislature, nor done many
unholy things that men have done; but
then we must remember that we have not
had the chance.

The good we secure for ourselves is
precarious and uncertain... until it is
secured for all of us and incorporated into
our common life.

You do not know what life means when
all the difficulties are removed! I am
simply smothered and sickened with

King

advantages. It is like eating a sweet dessert the first thing in the morning.

Jane Austen

[18th/19th Century British novelist]

I do not want people to be agreeable, as it saves me the trouble of liking them.

Where so many hours have been spent in convincing myself that I am right, is there not some reason to fear I may be wrong?

Janet Guthrie

[Aerospace engineer and the first woman to qualify and compete in both the Indianapolis 500 and the Daytona 500. The famed Smithsonian Institution houses her helmet and race suit]

Racing is a matter of spirit not strength. It is a matter of doing your best each little moment. There's never a break. You must have desire, a very intense desire to keep going.

You cannot afford to get angry behind the wheel. A good driver needs emotional detachment, concentration, good judgment, and desire.

Jean Driscoll

[American Gold Medal Paralympic champion; won the Boston Marathon, Wheelchair division eight times]

In wheelchair sports, people thought athletes with disabilities were courageous and inspirational. They never give them credit for simply being competitive.

Successful people are those who've fallen off the horse a dozen times and gotten back on a dozen times.

Jeane Kirkpatrick

[American professor, politician and first female U.S. Ambassador to the United Nations, 1981 to 1985]

A government is not legitimate merely because it exists.

Jeannette Rankin

[A socialist and pacifist; the first woman to be elected to the U. S. House of Representatives, 1917]

Go! Go! Go! It makes no difference where, just so you go! go! go! Remember at the first opportunity--go!

You can no more win a war than you can win an earthquake.

Joan Rivers

[American comedienne, actress and talk show host]

The first time I see a jogger smiling, I'll consider it.

Joan Benoit

Samuelson

[American marathon runner and the first female Olympic Gold Medal marathon champion, 1984]

I look at victory as milestones on a very long highway.

Joyce Maynard

[American author and professor]

A good home must be made, not bought.

Judith Martin

[American author, journalist and etiquette authority]

It is far more impressive when others discover your good qualities without your help.

Julia Louise Woodruff

[quotable author]

Out of the strain of the Doing, Into the peace of the Done.

Julie Krone

[First female jockey to win the Triple Crown]

I don't want to the be the best female jockey in the world; I want to be the best jockey.

I'm on top, I'm 35 years old, and there are other things I want to do. Physically, there is a lot of pain. I don't want to be hurt again. I have nothing left to prove.

Katharine Hepburn

[American actress of stage, television and film. With four Oscars, Hepburn has been recognized by the American Film Institute as the greatest female star in the history of American cinema]

Without discipline, there's no life at all.

Acting is the most minor of gifts and not a very high-class way to earn a living.

Katherine Mansfield

Risk! Risk anything! Care no more for the opinion of others, for those voices. Do the hardest thing on earth for you. Act for

[New Zealand modernist writer]

yourself. Face the truth.

Make it a rule of life never to regret and never to look back. Regret is an appalling waste of energy; you can't build on it; it's only for wallowing in.

Katharine Whitehorn

[British writer and columnist]

The easiest way for your children to learn about money is for you not to have any.

Kathleen Norris

[20th Century American novelist]

Before you begin a thing, remind yourself that difficulties and delays quite impossible to foresee are ahead. If you could see them clearly, naturally you could do a great deal to get rid of them but you can't. You can only see one thing clearly and that is your goal. Form a mental vision of that and cling to it through thick and thin.

Lady Bird Johnson

[First Lady of the White House from 1963 to 1969; wife to President Lyndon Baines Johnson, the 36th President of the United States]

It's odd that you can get so anesthetized by your own pain or your own problem that you don't quite fully share the hell of someone close to you.

The way you overcome shyness is to become so wrapped up in something that you forget to be afraid.

King

Lady Marguerite
Blessington
[18th Century
socialite and writer]

A woman's head is always influenced by heart; but a man's heart by his head.

Laurie Anderson
[American musician, singer, performance artist]

When love is gone, there's always justice. And when justice is gone, there's always force. And when force is gone, there's always Mom. Hi, Mom!

Lawana Blackwell

Age is no guarantee of maturity.

[American author]

I've grown to realize the joy that comes from little victories is preferable to the fun that comes from ease and the pursuit of pleasure.

If there was strife and contention in the home, very little else in life could compensate for it.

It isn't kind to cultivate a friendship just so one will have an audience.

Outings are so much more fun when we can savor them through the children's eyes.

Patterning your life around other's opinions is nothing more than slavery.

Leona Helmsley

[American business billionaire known as the "Queen of Mean"]

I don't hire people who have to be told to be nice. I hire nice people.

Lillian Hellman

[American playwright]

I cannot and will not cut my conscience to fit this year's fashions.

Lily Tomlin

[American comedian, writer and actor]

Man invented language to satisfy his deep need to complain.

Sometimes I worry about being a success in a mediocre world.

The trouble with the rat race is that even if you win, you're still a rat.

We're all in this alone.

Lisa Alther

[American author and novelist]

I happen to feel that the degree of a person's intelligence is directly reflected by the number of conflicting attitudes she can bring to bear on the same topic.

Liza Minnelli

[American singer and actress]

Reality is something you rise above.

Lois McMaster Bujold

[American science fiction writer]

If the truth doesn't save us, what does that say about us?

Louise Nevelson

[Ukrainian-born American artist]

A woman may not hit a ball stronger than a man, but it is different. I prize that difference.

I think all great innovations are built on rejections.

I think most artists create out of despair. The very nature of creation is not a performing glory on the outside, it's a painful, difficult search within.

What we call reality is an agreement that people have arrived at to make life more livable.

Lucille Ball

[Extremely popular American actress of film and television; comedian, model and business executive]

Love yourself first and everything else falls into line.

I'm not funny. What I am is brave.

One of the things I learned the hard way was that it doesn't pay to get discouraged.

Luck? I don't know anything about luck. I've never banked on it and I'm afraid of people who do. Luck to me is something else: hard work - and realizing what is opportunity and what isn't.

Lucille Ball	Keeping busy and making optimism a way of life can restore your faith in yourself. The secret of staying young is to live honestly, eat slowly, and lie about your age.

A man who correctly guesses a woman's age may be smart, but he's not very bright.

You really have to love yourself to get anything done in this world.

Knowing what you cannot do is more important than knowing what you can do. In fact, that's good taste.

I'd rather regret the things that I have done than (those) I have not.

Lucille S. Harper
[quotable author]

The nice thing about egotists is that they don't talk about other people.

Lydia M. Child
[19th Century American author, journalist, abolitionist and women's rights activist]

Genius hath electric power which earth can never tame.

Lynda Barry
[American author and cartoonist]

Love is an exploding cigar we willingly smoke.

Lucy Larcom

[19th Century
American poet]

If the world seems cold to you, kindle fires
to warm it.

Madam Curie

[Physicist and
chemist of Polish
decent; Nobel
Laureate, Physics,
1903 and Chemistry,
1911]

One never notices what has been done;
one can only see what remains to be done.

Madame de Tencin

[16th/17th Century
French author and
courtesan]

Never refuse any advance of friendship,
for if nine out of ten bring you nothing,
one alone may repay you.

Madeleine

Albright

[American diplomat
and the First female
United States
Secretary of State,
1997 to 2001]

While democracy in the long run is the
most stable form of government, in the
short run, it is among the most fragile.

To understand Europe, you have to be a
genius - or French.

I was a little girl in World War II and I'm
used to being freed by Americans.

Madeleine L'Engle

[American fiction
writer and poet]

To be alive is to be vulnerable.

The Age of the Female II: Heroines of the Shift

Mae West

[American actress of
stage, film, radio]

Too much of a good thing is wonderful.

You're never too old to become younger.

He who hesitates is a damned fool.

Mairead Corrigan

Maguire

[Nobel Peace Prize
co-recipient, 1977,
with Betty Williams]

If we want to reap the harvest of peace and
justice in the future, we will have to sow
the seeds of nonviolence, here and now, in
the present.

Margaret Bonnano

[Science fiction
writer]

It is only possible to live happily ever after
on a day-to-day basis.

Margaret Fuller

[19th Century
American journalist,
critic, teacher and
women's rights
activist]

If you have knowledge, let others light
their candles at it.

Men, for the sake of living, forget to live.

Male and female represent the two sides of
the great radical dualism. But in fact they
are perpetually passing into one another.
Fluid hardens to solid, solid rushes to
fluid. There is no wholly masculine man,
no purely feminine woman.

Margaret Mead

[American writer,
world-famous
anthropologist and
speaker]

It has been a woman's task throughout
history to go on believing in life when
there was almost no hope.

King

Margaret Mead

I have spent most of my life studying the lives of other peoples -- faraway peoples -- so that Americans might better understand themselves.

Mothers are a biological necessity; fathers are a social invention.

Women want mediocre men, and men are working to become as mediocre as possible.

There is no evidence that suggests women are naturally better at caring for children . . . with the fact of child-bearing out of the center of attention, there is even more reason for treating girls first as human beings, then as women.

The male form of a female liberationist is a male liberationist — a man who realizes the unfairness of having to work all his life to support a wife and children so that someday his widow may live in comfort, a man who points out that commuting to a job he doesn't like is just as oppressive as his wife's imprisonment in a suburb, a man who rejects his exclusion, by society and most women, from participation in

childbirth and the most engrossing,
delightful care of young children — a
man, in fact, who wants to relate himself
to people and the world around him as a
person.

If we are to achieve a richer culture, rich
in contrasting values, we must recognize
the whole gamut of human potentialities.
We must weave a social fabric in which
each diverse human gift will find a fitting
place.

We are living beyond our means. As a
people we have developed a life-style that
is draining the earth of its priceless and
irreplaceable resources without regard for
the future of our children and people all
around the world.

Never doubt that a small, group of
thoughtful, committed citizens can change
the world. Indeed, it is the only thing that
ever has.

We women are doing pretty well. We're
almost back to where we were in the
twenties.

King

242

Margaret Millar

[Canadian born author or suspense and mystery]

Most conversations are simply monologues delivered in the presence of witnesses.

Margaret Mitchell

[Pulitzer Prize winning American author, 1937, for *Gone with the Wind*]

Until you've lost your reputation, you never realize what a burden it was.

There ain't nothing from the outside that can lick any of us.

Life's under no obligation to give us what we expect.

Margaret Smith Court

[Famous world renowned Australian tennis player]

My femininity is always something I've tried to preserve in this dog-eat-dog world.

Margaret Thatcher

[Prime Minister of Great Britain from 1979 to 1990; known as the "Iron Lady" in respect for her toughness]

We want a society where people are free to make choices, to make mistakes, to be generous and compassionate. This is what we mean by a moral society; not a society where the state is responsible for everything, and no one is responsible for the state.

If you want anything said, ask a man. If you want something done, ask a woman. If you just set out to be liked, you would

be prepared to compromise on anything at
any time, and you would achieve nothing.

I do not know anyone who has got to the
top without hard work. That is the recipe.
It will not always get you to the top, but
should get you pretty near.

If you want to cut your own throat, don't
come to me for a bandage.

Pennies do not come from heaven. They
have to be earned here on earth.

Disciplining yourself to do what you know
is right and important, although difficult,
is the highroad to pride, self-esteem, and
personal satisfaction.

Being powerful is like being a lady. If you
have to tell people you are, you aren't.

You may have to fight a battle more than
once to win it.

I'm extraordinarily patient provided I get
my own way in the end.

Of course it's the same old story. Truth
usually is the same old story.

King

Margaret Thatcher

To wear your heart on your sleeve isn't a very good plan; you should wear it inside, where it functions best.

I have always said if you want a speech, ask a man. If you want something done, ask a woman.

Margery Allingham

[English author and novelist in mystery and crime genres]

When the habitually even-tempered suddenly fly into a passion, that explosion is apt to be more impressive than the outburst of the most violent amongst us.

Margo Kaufman

[American writer and humorist]

The only thing worse than a man you can't control is a man you can.

Maria Mitchell

[19th Century American astronomer]

Besides learning to see, there is another art to be learned--not to see what is not.

Maria Montessori

[Italian physician and educator; Founder of the Montessori method of education]

Never help a child with a task at which he feels he can succeed.

Marianne Williamson

[American author, lecturer, spiritual activist and founder of The Peace Alliance]

Spiritual progress is like detoxification. Things have to come up in order to be released. Once we have asked to be healed, then our unhealed places are forced to the surface.

The practice of forgiveness is our most important contribution to the healing of the world.

Marilyn Ferguson

[American author, speaker and editor]

Of all the self-fulfilling prophecies in our culture, the assumption that aging means decline and poor health is probably the deadliest.

Marilyn Milian

[Of Cuban descent, Judge Milian is the first female to preside over *The People's Court* television show]

Don't give cash with this hand without getting a receipt in this one!

I wouldn't believe you if your tongue came notarized. OK?

Marilyn Monroe

[Famous American actress and sex siren icon of Hollywood fame]

Hollywood is a place where they'll pay you a thousand dollars for a kiss and fifty cents for your soul.

My work is the only ground I've ever had to stand on. I seem to have a whole superstructure with no foundation--but I'm working on the foundation.

King

I want to be a big star more than anything.
It's something precious.

Marlene Dietrich

[American actress
and singer of
German descent]

I love quotations because it is a joy to find
thoughts one might have, beautifully
expressed with much authority by
someone recognized wiser than oneself.

Most women set out to try to change a
man, and when they have changed him
they don't like him.

Once a woman has forgiven her man, she
must not reheat his sins for breakfast.

Martha Graham

[American dancer,
choreographer and
pioneer of modern
dance]

The body is a sacred garment.

Martina

Navratilova

[Famous former
World #1 tennis star
of Czechoslovakian
descent]

The moment of victory is much too short
to live for that and nothing else.

Just go out there and do what you've got to
do.

Mary Daly

[American feminist
philosopher and
theologian]

It is the creative potential itself in human
beings that is the image of God.

Mary Hemingway

[American journalist. She was also the widow and fourth wife of author Ernest Hemingway]

Worry a little bit every day and in a lifetime you will lose a couple of years. If something is wrong, fix it if you can, but train yourself not to worry. Worry never fixes anything.

Mary Hirsch

[American humorist and writer]

Humor is a rubber sword - it allows you to make a point without drawing blood.

Mary Howitt

[19th Century English poet]

Visions come not to polluted eyes.

Mary Jean LeTendre

[U.S. Department of Education public servant]

Let us never confuse stability for stagnation.

Mary Kay Ash

[American entrepreneur and founder of May Kay Cosmetics]

If you think you can, you can, and if you think you can't, you're right.

People fail forward to success.

Mary MacCracken

[American writer]

Level with your child by being honest. Nobody spots a phony quicker than a child.

Mary McLeod
Bethune
[American civil
rights leader and
educator]

For I am my mother's daughter, and the drums of Africa still beat in my heart.

They will not let me rest while there is a single Negro boy or girl without a chance to prove his worth.

Maureen Dowd
[Pulitzer Prize
winning American
reporter, columnist]

The minute you settle for less than you deserve, you get even less than you settled for.

Maureen Murphy
[American politician
and 1st district
Commissioner of the
Cook County Board
of Review, Illinois]

The reason there are so few female politicians is that it is too much trouble to put makeup on two faces.

Meryl Streep
[American actress of
film, television and
theater]

You can't get spoiled if you do your own ironing.

Mia Hamm
[American icon of
female soccer]

No-one gets an iron-clad guarantee of success.

Mignon
McLaughlin
[American author
and journalist]

There are so many things that we wish we had done yesterday, so few that we feel like doing today.

Millicent Fenwick

[American politician, diplomat and fashion editor]

Never feel self-pity, the most destructive emotion there is. How awful to be caught up in the terrible squirrel cage of self.

Mother Teresa

[Albanian Roman Catholic nun, Nobel Peace Laureate, 1979, and world-renowned humanitarian of the poor and helpless]

I know God will not give me anything I can't handle. I just wish that He didn't trust me so much.

Let no one ever come to you without leaving better and happier.

Let us make one point, that we meet each other with a smile, when it is difficult to smile. Smile at each other, make time for each other in your family.

Do not wait for leaders; do it alone, person to person.

Muriel Lester

[British social reformer and pacifist]

The job of the peacemaker is to stop war, to purify the world, to get it saved from poverty and riches, to heal the sick, to comfort the sad, to wake up those who have not yet found God.

Nadia Comaneci

[Romanian gymnast, scoring the first perfect score of 10.0 on the uneven bars.]

Hard work has made it easy. That is my secret. That is why I win.

King

Nancy Lopez

[American golfer]

I love the challenge.

Olga Korbut

[Olympic Gold Medal Soviet gymnast, 1972, Munich]

Don't be afraid if things seem difficult in the beginning. That's only the initial impression. The important thing is not to retreat; you have to master yourself.

Oprah Winfrey

[American media icon, actress, talk show host and billionaire entrepreneur]

Surround yourself with only people who are going to lift you higher.

Follow your instincts. That's where true wisdom manifests itself.

Real integrity is doing the right thing, knowing that nobody's going to know whether you did it or not.

Think like a queen. A queen is not afraid to fail. Failure is another steppingstone to greatness.

Where there is no struggle, there is no strength.

Excellence is the best deterrent to racism or sexism.

My philosophy is that not only are you responsible for your life, but doing the best at this moment puts you in the best place for the next moment.

I always knew I was destined for greatness.

The more you praise and celebrate your life, the more there is in life to celebrate.

I am a woman in process. I'm just trying like everybody else. I try to take every conflict, every experience, and learn from it. Life is never dull.

I do not believe in failure. It is not failure if you enjoyed the process.

Turn your wounds into wisdom.

We can't become what we need to be by remaining what we are.

If you come to fame not understanding who you are, it will define who you are.

It isn't until you come to a spiritual understanding of who you are - not necessarily a religious feeling, but deep down, the spirit within - that you can begin to take control.

King

Oprah Winfrey

Lots of people want to ride with you in the limo, but what you want is someone who will take the bus with you when the limo breaks down.

You are what you are by what you believe!

Patricia Moyes

[Irish-born British mystery writer]

I simply cannot understand the passion that some people have for making themselves thoroughly uncomfortable and then boasting about it afterwards.

Patricia Neal

[American actress]

A strong positive mental attitude will create more miracles than any wonder drug.

Patricia Sampson

[quotable author]

Self-reliance is the only road to true freedom, and being one's own person is its ultimate reward.

Patti Weekes

[American educator]

Today is the culmination of my entire life.

Pearl Bailey

[American singer, dancer and actress]

The first and worst of all frauds is to cheat one's self. All sin is easy after that.

A man without ambition is dead. A man with ambition but no love is dead. A man with ambition and love for his blessings here on earth is ever so alive. Having been alive, it won't be so hard in the end to lie down and rest.

There's a period of life when we swallow a knowledge of ourselves and it becomes either good or sour inside.

What the world really needs is more love and less paper work.

Pearl S. Buck

[The first American woman to receive the Nobel Prize for literature (1938); Pulitzer Prize recipient in 1932]

A good marriage is one which allows for change and growth in the individuals and in the way they express their love.

Order is the shape upon which beauty depends.

It is better to be first with an ugly woman than the hundredth with a beauty.

None who have always been free can understand the terrible fascinating power of the hope of freedom to those who are not free.

One faces the future with one's past.

King

254

Peggy Fleming

[Olympic Champion,
Ice Skating, 1968,
Grenoble, France]

The first thing is to love your sport. Never do it to please someone else. It has to be yours.

Phyllis Diller

[American
comedian]

Always be nice to your children because they are the ones who will choose your rest home.

Never go to bed mad. Stay up and fight.

Phyllis Mcginley

[American writer
and poet]

A hobby a day keeps the doldrums away.

Princess Diana

[International British
icon, Queen of
Hearts, the People's
Princess and former
Princess of Wales]

Being a princess isn't all it's cracked up to be.

I understand people's suffering, people's pain, more than you will ever know yourself.

I am not a political figure, nor do I want to be one; but I come with my heart.

I wear my heart on my sleeve.

Princess Tenko

[Japanese magician
and former pop
singer]

Do what you think is best for you and follow your dreams. Don't listen to negative comments from anyone else. When you decide on something, just go straight for it and keep at it until you get it.

Queen Margrethe II of Denmark
I have always had a dread of becoming a passenger in life.

Rita Holt
[American author]
There it was, hidden in alphabetical order.

Rita Mae Brown
[American author, novelist, poet and screenwriter]
One of the keys to happiness is a bad memory.

The statistics on sanity are that one out of every four Americans is suffering from some form of mental illness. Think of your three best friends. If they're okay, then it's you.

A life of reaction is a life of slavery, intellectually and spirituality. One must fight for a life of action, not reaction.

Rita Rudner
[American comedian, writer and actress]
Before I met my husband, I'd never fallen in love, though I'd stepped in it a few times.

I got kicked out of ballet class because I pulled a groin muscle. It wasn't mine.

I love being married. It's so great to find

Rita Rudner

that one special person you want to annoy for the rest of your life.

I was a vegetarian until I started leaning toward the sunlight.

I was going to have cosmetic surgery until I noticed that the doctor's office was full of portraits by Picasso.

I wonder if other dogs think poodles are members of a weird religious cult.

In Hollywood a marriage is a success if it outlasts milk.

My husband gave me a necklace. It's fake. I requested fake. Maybe I'm paranoid, but in this day and age, I don't want something around my neck that's worth more than my head.

Rosalynn Carter

[First Lady of the United States; wife of Jimmy Carter, 39th President]

You have to have confidence in your ability, and then be tough enough to follow through.

Rosa Parks

[African-American
civil rights activist
who sparked the
Montgomery,
Alabama, Bus
Boycott on
December 1, 1955]

I believe that we are here on the planet
Earth to live, grow up and do what we can
to make this world a better place for all
people to enjoy freedom.

I was determined to achieve the total
freedom that our history lessons taught us
we were entitled to, no matter what the
sacrifice.

Memories of our lives, of our works and
our deeds will continue in others.

I have learned over the years that when
one's mind is made up, this diminishes
fear; knowing what must be done does
away with fear.

Sally Kristen Ride

[Physicist, astronaut,
and the first
American woman in
outer space, 1983]

All adventures, especially into new
territory, are scary.

Sandra Day
O'Connor

[First female Justice
of the Supreme
Court of the United
States (1981 to
2006)]

A moment of silence is not inherently
religious.

Do the best you can in every task, no
matter how unimportant it may seem at the
time. No one learns more about a problem

King

Sandra Day
O'Conner

than the person at the bottom.

It is difficult to discern a serious threat to religious liberty from a room of silent, thoughtful schoolchildren.

The power I exert on the court depends on the power of my arguments, not on my gender.

Despite the encouraging and wonderful gains and the changes for women which have occurred in my lifetime, there is still room to advance and to promote correction of the remaining deficiencies and imbalances.

The family unit plays a critical role in our society and in the training of the generation to come.

Shirley Lord

[American author and journalist]

What really matters is what you do with what you have.

Shirley MacLaine

[American actress, dancer, author and spiritual activist]

Dwelling on the negative simply contributes to its power.

Shirley Temple

[American actress and iconic child star]

I stopped believing in Santa Claus when my mother took me to see him in a department store, and he asked for my autograph.

Sophia Loren

[Italian film actress]

Getting ahead in a difficult profession requires avid faith in yourself. That is why some people with mediocre talent, but with great inner drive, go much farther than people with vastly superior talent.

St. Catherine of Siena

[14th Century Roman Catholic Saint]

In mercy you have seen fit today to show me, poor as I am, how we can in no way pass judgment on other people's intentions.

St. Claire of Assisi

[12th Century Roman Catholic Saint]

Go forth in peace, for you have followed the good road. Go forth without fear, for He that created you has sanctified you, has always protected you, and loves you as a mother.

Stella Benson

[British writer, novelist, feminist]

Call no man foe, but never love a stranger.

SuEllen Fried

[Author and international speaker against child abuse and bullying]

It is no sin to attempt and fail. The only sin is not to make the attempt.

King

Susan B. Anthony

[Prominent leader in the women's suffrage movement; her image was the first real woman on a U.S. coin - The Susan B. Anthony dollar, introduced in 1979]

Cautious, careful people, always casting about to preserve their reputations... can never effect a reform.

Failure is impossible.

It was we, the people; not we, the white male citizens; nor yet we, the male citizens; but we, the whole people, who formed the Union... Men, their rights and nothing more; women, their rights and nothing less.

Resolved, that the women of this nation in 1876, have greater cause for discontent, rebellion and revolution than the men of 1776.

Suffrage is the pivotal right.

Susan Ertz

[British writer and novelist]

Millions long for immortality who don't know what to do on a rainy day.

Susan J. Bissonette

[quotable author]

An optimist is the human personification of spring.

Suzanne Gordon

[journalist, author and health advocate]

To be alone is to be different; to be different is to be alone.

The Age of the Female II: Heroines of the Shift

Suzanne Necker

[18th Century
French patroness]

Fortune does not change men, it unmasks them.

Tallulah Bankhead

[American actress
and talk show host]

I'm as pure as the driven slush.

It's the good girls who keep diaries; the bad girls never have the time.

Nobody can be exactly like me. Sometimes even I have trouble doing it.

If I had to live my life again, I'd make the same mistakes, only sooner.

Toni Morrison

[American author,
editor, professor and
Nobel Laureate,
Literature, 1993;
Pulitzer Prize, 1988]

If there's a book you really want to read, but it hasn't been written yet, then you must write it.

If you're going to hold someone down, you're going to have to hold on by the other end of the chain. You are confined by your own repression.

Tracy Caulkins

[American Gold
Medal swimmer,
1984 Olympics, Los
Angeles]

I know a lot of people think it's monotonous, down the black lines over and over, but it's not if you're enjoying what you're doing. I love to swim and I love to train.

King

Willa Cather

[American author
and novelist]

What was any art but an effort to make a
sheath, a mold in which to imprison for a
moment the shining, elusive element
which is life itself.

I tell you there is such a thing as creative
hate.

A child's attitude toward everything is an
artist's attitude.

Wilma Rudolph

[American Olympic
Gold Medalist in
track and field, 1960,
Rome, Italy]

From that day on, people were going to
start separating me from that brace, start
thinking about me differently, start saying
[she] is a healthy kid, just like the rest of
them.

I ran and ran and ran every day, and I
acquired this sense of determination, this
sense of spirit that I would never, never
give up, no matter what else happened.

My mother taught me very early to believe
I could achieve any accomplishment I
wanted to. The first was to walk without
braces.

Wislawa

Szymborska

[Polish poet, essayist and translator. Nobel Laureate, Literature, 1996]

In every tragedy, an element of comedy is preserved. Comedy is just tragedy reversed.

Even the worst book can give us something to think about.

Zora Neale

Hurston

[American author, and folklorist of the Harlem Renaissance era]

Mama exhorted her children at every opportunity to 'jump at de sun.' We might not land on the sun, but at least we would get off the ground.

Zsa Zsa Gabor

[Hungarian-born American actress and socialite]

Macho does not prove mucho.

Husbands are like fires. They go out if unattended.

The Age of the Female II: Heroines of the Shift

RICHARD ANDREW KING – BOOKS
www.RichardKing.net/Books

The Age of the Female
A Thousand Years of Yin

AOF I highlights the profound and extraordinary ascent of the female in the modern world, placing her center stage in the global spotlight as presidents and leaders of nations, titans of industry, corporate executives, military generals, media magnets, doctors, lawyers and a whole host of other prestigious titles normally associated with the male. Why has her rise to prominence been so rapid, especially in consideration of historic time? Why also has there been an increased interest in other people's lives in our society, in competitive athletics, personal data collection and the exploration of space and other worlds? *The Age of the Female: A Thousand Years of Yin* answers these questions. It is an insightful and exciting read into these mysteries, offering compelling and irrefutable evidence through the ancient science and art of numerology that, indeed, the age of the female has arrived and the next thousand years belong, not to him, but to her.

The Age of the Female II
Heroines of the Shift

AOF II continues the remarkable journey of the female's ascent in the modern world of the 2nd Millennium. This installment is a general read in five chapters honoring the accomplishments of women in categories of female firsts, female Nobel laureates, female athletes, female icons and female quotations. The achievements of the women featured in *The Age of the Female II; Heroines of the Shift* are deserving of respect and admiration. Their lives, challenges and successes are motivational catalysts for every individual to be the best he or she can be and to honor the very essence of what it is to be human. *The Age of the Female II; Heroines of the Shift* is intended to be an inspiring and educational read for everyone, not just women but men, too, offering knowledge and insight of the depth, power and daring-do of women as their Yin energy rises upon the global stage in this millennium which destiny has irrefutably marked as the Age of the Female.

The King's Book of Numerology
Volume 1-Foundations & Fundamentals

KBN 1 provides complete descriptions of Basic Numbers, Double Numbers, Purifier Numbers, Master Numbers, the Letters in Simple and Specific form as well as the Basic Matrix, the numerological blueprint of our lives.

"*The King's Book of Numerology* contains new information that informs and predicts more completely and accurately than any previously published numerological work. It brings back the empowered sciences of long ago, information long since lost upon this plane." ~G. Shaver

"The best numerology book I've ever read." M.W.

The King's Book of Numerology II
Forecasting - Part 1

KBN 2 is dedicated to opening the door to the divine blueprint of our lives. That plan, that divine blueprint of destiny, is exact, precise, unchangeable, unalterable and . . . knowable, at least in general terms. Once this awareness of a predetermined fate becomes established through application of numbers and their truths, our understanding and consciousness of life will, no doubt, change. We will begin to see ourselves as part of an immense spiritual super-structure far beyond our current ability to comprehend, understand or perceive. Life will take on new meaning and, perhaps, we will even begin to awaken to greater spiritual truths. Subjects covered: Life Cycle Patterns, The Pinnacle/Challenge Matrix, Epoch Timeline, Voids, Case Studies.

Blueprint of a Princess
Diana Frances Spencer - Queen of Hearts

The tragic death of Princess Diana of Wales - the most famous, the most photographed, the most written about woman of the modern world and possibly of all time - was one of the most shocking and saddening events of the late Twentieth Century. Not since the assassination of American President John Fitzgerald Kennedy in 1963, has such an event captured the attention of the world. On that ill-fated Sunday of 31 August 1997, and the following week until her funeral, there was much discussion and reflection of the Queen of Hearts, the People's Princess, England's Rose. But in all of the media news coverage, there was no discussion given to the cosmic aspects of her life and death. This book is dedicated to addressing those issues through The King's Numerology. Its purpose and hope is to offer some consolation and

The Age of the Female II: Heroines of the Shift

explanation as to that one question so poignantly written on a card of condolence left with the multitude of flowers before the gates of Buckingham Palace. . . "Why?"

99 Poems of the Spirit

99 Poems of the Spirit draws from the writings of Perfect Saints, Masters, Mystics and Sacred Scriptures, encompassing a wide range of spiritual topics in poetic form: *karma, reincarnation, transmigration, destiny, devotion, vegetarianism, attainment, the human form, love, morality, heaven, hell, the inner regions, justice the nature of this world, illusion, deception, success, money, the Pendulum, the struggle between this world and the higher worlds and much, much more.*

The selections within *99 Poems of the Spirit* are designed to lift the mind, heart and consciousness, allowing the individual to connect with the mystic side of life in order to enhance the process of self-realization while advancing on the spiritual path and climbing the ladder leading to the ultimate attainment of God Realization.

All of the selections in *99 Poems of the Spirit* are original works by Richard Andrew King. If you like poetry and spiritual food for thought, then this is a book you want to read and have in your personal library. It is a treasure chest of poetic spiritual gems offered to excite, educate and stimulate the mind and soul in the glorious journey of spiritual ascent.

Messages from the Masters
Timeless Truths for Spiritual Seekers

In a time where there is more need for enlightenment than ever before, *Messages from the Masters* offers timeless truths for genuine seekers thirsty for spiritual nectar.

Masters are the PhDs of the universe, the Light Bearers of the Divine Flame. Their knowledge and wisdom are supreme. They have no equal. Although appearing human, they are not. Masters are the exalted Sons of God. Their chief duty is to rescue souls, liberating them from the maniacal maelstrom and madness of the material world and returning them to their eternal Home with the Lord.

Messages from the Masters is a rich source of hundreds of quotes from a cavalcade of nine Perfect Saints throughout the last six hundred years: Guru Ravidas, Kabir, Guru Nanak, Tulsi Sahib, Swami Ji Maharaj, Baba Jaimal Singh, Sawan Singh, Jagat Singh and Charan Singh. The messages in this

King

book focus on the importance of the Divine Diet, the priceless Human Form, Reincarnation, the World, the Negative Power and Soul Food.

Warning! *Messages from the Masters* is not for the faint of heart or the worldly-minded. Masters come into the world to sever our attachment to it, not make it a paradise. Although the epitome of love and wisdom, they shoot straight from the hip, pull no punches, favor no religion. Their universal message of soul liberation is reflected in the statement of Saint Maharaj Charan Singh: *Just live in the creation and get out of it*!

Your Love Numbers
Discovering the Secrets of Your Life, Loves, and Relationships

Your Love Numbers reveals the secret formula defining all great relationships and how to assess the love potential of any relationship.

Your Love Numbers reveals the mystery of love through the most ancient of all sciences . . . numbers, your numbers, calculated using only your full name and date of birth and those of the people you love! "Numbers rule the universe; everything is arranged according to number and mathematical shape," said Pythagoras. And, yes, everything, including love, can be measured in numbers!

Your Love Numbers is based on research by master numerologist, Richard Andrew King. Applying his unique and revolutionary new theories, love and attraction between people can be determined using very easy to learn concepts. With a little study and practice, all this can be done in a matter of minutes.

Your Love Numbers teaches you how to assess a relationship or potential relationship in minutes, saving you endless time, energy, effort and possible heartache in the end. By knowing ourselves and the people we love, our relationships will be potentially more rewarding, satisfying, productive, peaceful, lasting and loving . . . for everyone - our family, spouses, partners, children, friends.

YourLoveNumbers.com

Destinies of the Rich & Famous
The Secret Numbers of Extraordinary Lives

Why are rich and famous people rich and famous? Is it luck? Hard work? Advantage by family name? What makes them special? What secrets are the basis of their success?

Why is Oprah Winfrey a billionaire entrepreneur?
What gives Sarah Palin her Going Rogue persona?
What caused Marilyn Monroe to be a sex goddess?
What caused Princess Diana's tragic life and death?
Why was Michael Jackson plagued by child issues?
Why was Howard Hughes a disturbed, rich recluse?

Destinies of the Rich & Famous explores the secret numbers of the following famous global icons and explains through The King's Numerologytm why they are both rich and famous.

Dr. Albert Einstein - Amelia Earhart - Elvis Presley - General George Patton - Howard Hughes - John F. Kennedy - Marilyn Monroe - Michael Jackson - Muhammad Ali - Oprah Winfrey - Princess Diana - Sarah Palin

DestiniesOfTheRichAndFamous.com

Parenting Wisdom
What To Teach The Children

Parenting Wisdom – What To Teach The Children is a companion book to *Parenting Wisdom For The 21st Century – Raising Your Children By Their Numbers To Achieve Their Highest Potential.*

Parenting Wisdom supports parents in their most important and critical job in life – the cultivating and sculpting of children.

In the process of parenting one of the most germane questions is, "What do we teach the children?" Parenting Wisdom offers thirty-three time-tested, universal principles which parents can use to create a strong foundation allowing children to develop into whole, fulfilled, and substantive adults.

The thirty-three principles include:

The Five Needs of Children
Boundaries, Rules, And Regs

King

Your Life, Your Responsibility
Tender Love Versus Tough Love
The Four Cornerstones of a Substantive Life
The Temptations of S.A.D. (Sex, Alcohol, Drugs) and more . . .

As a father, grandfather, professional educator, and martial arts instructor, Richard Andrew King shares personal strategies in Parenting Wisdom which he has successfully used in the critically important function of sculpting strong, independent, and balanced children en route to becoming successful and substantive adults.

ParentingWisdom.net

Parenting Wisdom for the 21st Century
Raising Your Children By Their Numbers
To Achieve Their Highest Potential

This book is a must for any parent and all parents to be. It is vital to read this book now before you name your children. If you already have children, then it is just as important to understand them. Richard Andrew King should be called Dr. King. His books are of the magnitude that will be read with reverence for generations to come. ~ Dr. Victoria Ford, J.D.

Parenting Wisdom for the 21st Century - Raising Your Children by Their Numbers to Achieve Their Highest Potential is a revolutionary addition to the process of arguably the most important job in the world, parenting.

Master Numerologist, father and grandfather Richard Andrew King teaches you the secrets to understanding your children's destinies through the most ancient of all sciences, numbers.

The powerful information contained within this work will reveal the hidden desires driving your children, the paths they will follow in life, the roles they will give on the great life stage and much more – all designed to augment your parenting wisdom and support life's paramount parental purpose . . . to love the children and help them achieve their highest potential.

ParentingWisdom.net

The Age of the Female II: Heroines of the Shift

The Black Belt Book of Life
Secrets of a Martial Arts Master

The Black Belt Book of Life highlights forty foundational principles for creating a masterful, successful life, not just for martial artists but for everyone, adults and children alike.

The mystery and mystique of the martial arts is not only ages old, it's legend. Revered throughout the world, martial arts is a treasure chest of life secrets that transcend the boundaries of combat to include the expanse of life and living. Arguably, it is the greatest developmental system on earth for teaching the integration of body, mind and spirit.

The Black Belt Book of Life is not about physical fighting strategies and tactics. It is about concepts and principles we learn though martial arts training that can help us in the struggle of life, in the journey to conquer ourselves and gain the golden ring of our own completeness because in the end a true Black Belt should be a realized soul who, having engaged the enemy - himself - finds himself at the end of the journey . . . triumphant.

The Black Belt Book of Life reveals many secrets of martial arts training, sharing these truths in quick and easy to read vignettes to benefit martial artists and the general public as well. It is a book for all readers, not just martial artists, both males and females, especially the youth of today who are in search of a foundation to guide their lives.

The Galactic Transcripts

It's the 1950s. A man sees a cigar-shaped UFO, subsequently becomes involved in receiving channeled messages from intergalactic "human" beings, and then, within hours of his death, writes *Border to Infinity* as the final entry in his personal journal. What does it all mean? And could these events be interconnected?

The Galactic Transcripts will take you on a journey that is as provocative as it is mysterious. Its thirty-seven transmissions are channeled from a non-earth, alien group who identify themselves as members of the Space Brotherhood – messages imparted by representatives known as Monka, Korton, Traenor, Klala, Hatton, Lalur, and Soltec.

Learn what the Space Brotherhood also has to say about other organizations such as the Galactic Counsel, Confederation of Galaxies, Counsel of Lords, Solar Tribunal, and Solar Cross Foundation.

King

The Galactic Transcripts offer us descriptions of other worlds, their inhabitants, morals, ethics, and histories. They even forewarn of the coming cleansing of earth and the cataclysms preceding it. Other messages shed light on the original colonization of earth, telepathic communication, the power of love, the program of the Radiant One, and much more.

Those who have read *The Galactic Transcripts* have found them to be life-altering, profound, inspirational, transformative. Will they have that effect on you? Open your mind and allow the transcripts to take you beyond the limitations of our world and into new, undiscovered worlds far beyond our galaxy.

TheGalacticTranscripts.com

The Age of the Female II: Heroines of the Shift

References

[1] http://womenshistory.about.com/od/quotes/a/jane_addams.htm

[2] http://www.umkc.edu/imc/womenfi.htm

[3] http://www.umkc.edu/imc/womenfi.htm

[4] http://www.umkc.edu/imc/womenfi.htm

[5] http://www.umkc.edu/imc/womenfi.htm

[6] http://www.umkc.edu/imc/womenfi.htm

[7] http://www.umkc.edu/imc/womenfi.htm

[8] http://www.nobel.se/peace/laureates/1931/addams-bio.html

[9] http://www.umkc.edu/imc/index.html

[10] http://www.umkc.edu/imc/index.html

[11] http://www.umkc.edu/imc/index.html

[12] http://www.umkc.edu/imc/index.html

[13] http://womenshistory.about.com/cs/bandaranaike/

[14] http://www.distinguishedwomen.com/biographies/gleason.html

[15] http://www.thewhitehouseproject.org/know_facts/women_firsts.html

[16] http://www.huntington.org/vfw/imp/rankin.html

[17] http://www.umkc.edu/imc/womenfi.htm

[18] http://www.thewhitehouseproject.org/know_facts/women_firsts.html

[19] http://www.ninety-nines.org/coleman.html

[20] http://www.umkc.edu/imc/womenfi.htm

[21] http://www.umkc.edu/imc/womenfi.htm

[22] http://www.umkc.edu/imc/womenfi.htm

[23] http://www.thewhitehouseproject.org/know_facts/women_firsts.html

[24] http://www.umkc.edu/imc/womenfi.htm

[25] http://www.umkc.edu/imc/womenfi.htm

[26] http://www.umkc.edu/imc/womenfi.htm

[27] http://www.umkc.edu/imc/womenfi.htm

[28] http://www.ameliaearhart.com/achievements.html
http://ellensplace.net/ae_eyrs.html

[29] http://www.sciencemuseum.org.uk/collections/exhiblets/johnson/start.asp

[30] http://www.umkc.edu/imc/womenfi.htm

[31] http://www.ushistory.net/toc/addams.html

[32] http://www.flightlinemalta.com

[33] http://www.senate.gov/~lincoln/html/hattaway.html

[34] http://www.ssa.gov/history/fperkins.html

[35] http://www.umkc.edu/imc/womenfi.htm

[36] http://www.thewhitehouseproject.org/know_facts/women_firsts.html

[37] http://www.encyclopedia.com/html/C/ConnollyM1.asp

[38] http://www.flightlinemalta.com

[39] http://www.dailycelebrations.com/031401.htm

[40] http://www.nasm.si.edu/nasm/aero/women_aviators/jackie_cochran.htm

[41] http://www.pulitzer.org

[42] http://www.umkc.edu/imc/womenfi.htm

[43] http://www.thewhitehouseproject.org/know_facts/women_firsts.html

[44] http://www.umkc.edu/imc/womenfi.htm

[45] http://www.thewhitehouseproject.org/know_facts/women_firsts.html

[46] http://www.thewhitehouseproject.org/know_facts/women_firsts.html

[47] http://www.thewhitehouseproject.org/know_facts/women_firsts.html

48 http://www.umkc.edu/imc/womenfi.htm
49 http://www.umkc.edu/imc/womenfi.htm
50 http://www.umkc.edu/imc/womenfi.htm
51 http://www.geocities.com/dblimbrick/gibson.html
52 http://www.umkc.edu/imc/womenfi.htm
53 http://espn.go.com/sportscentury/features/00016444.html
54 http://www.astronautix.com/astros/terhkova.htm
55 http://www.flughafengallery.com/Women/hub_www_jmock_5.htm
56 http://www.umkc.edu/imc/womenfi.htm
57 http://www.umkc.edu/imc/womenfi.htm
58 http://www.umkc.edu/imc/womenfi.htm
59 http://www.thewhitehouseproject.org/know_facts/women_firsts.html
60 http://www.thewhitehouseproject.org/know_facts/women_firsts.html
61 http://afgen.com/chisholm.html
62 http://www.womenssportsfoundation.org/cgi-
bin/iowa/issues/rights/article.html?record=752
63 http://history.amedd.army.mil/ANCWebsite/13_Hays.html
64 http://www.umkc.edu/imc/womenfi.htm
65 http://www.thewhitehouseproject.org/know_facts/women_firsts.html
66 http://www.military.com/Content/MoreContent?file=ML_duerk_bkp
67 http://www.beejae.com/bjordan.htm
68 http://www.thewhitehouseproject.org/know_facts/women_firsts.html
69 http://www.thewhitehouseproject.org/know_facts/women_firsts.html
70 http://www.thewhitehouseproject.org/know_facts/women_firsts.html
71 http://www.thewhitehouseproject.org/know_facts/women_firsts.html
72 http://www.umkc.edu/imc/womenfi.htm
73 http://www.janetguthrie.com/
74 http://www.britannia.com/gov/primes/prime56.html
75 http://www.geocities.com/zzbbelk/sbanthonydollarhistory.htm
76 http://www.thewhitehouseproject.org/know_facts/women_firsts.html
77 http://www.wic.org/bio/wvaught.htm
http://www.af.mil/news/biographies/vaught_wl.html
78 http://www.lucidcafe.com/library/96mar/oconnor.html
79 http://www2.lucidcafe.com/lucidcafe/library/96may/ride.html
80 http://www.library.okstate.edu/about/awards/winners/mankill.htm
81 http://www.thewhitehouseproject.org/know_facts/women_firsts.html
82 http://www.umkc.edu/imc/womenfi.htm
83 http://www.thewhitehouseproject.org/know_facts/women_firsts.html
84 http://www.alaska.net/~lriddles
85 http://www.time.com/time/special/moy/1986.html
86 http://inter-speak.com/butcher.htm
87 http://www.jsc.nasa.gov/Bios/htmlbios/mcauliffe.html
88 http://www.thewhitehouseproject.org/know_facts/women_firsts.html
89 http://www.thewhitehouseproject.org/know_facts/women_firsts.html
90 http://www.umkc.edu/imc/womenfi.htm
91 http://www.thewhitehouseproject.org/know_facts/women_firsts.html
92 http://www.thewhitehouseproject.org/know_facts
93 http://www.thewhitehouseproject.org/know_facts/women_firsts.html
94 http://www.umkc.edu/imc/womenfi.htm
95 http://www.topblacks.com/science/mae-jemison.htm

The Age of the Female II: Heroines of the Shift

[96] http://www.thewhitehouseproject.org/know_facts/women_firsts.html
[97] http://hall.racingmuseum.org/jockey.asp?ID=351
[98] http://www.thewhitehouseproject.org/know_facts/women_firsts.html
[99] http://www.black-collegian.com/african/1st-female-pilot.shtml
[100] http://www.umkc.edu/imc/womenfi.htm
[101] http://www.womeninaviation.com
[102] http://www.af.mil/news/Jul1998/n19980723_981078.html
[103] http://www.nobel.se/nobel/index.html
[104] http://www.nobel.se/nobel/alfred-nobel/index.html
[105] http://www.nobel.se/nobel/alfred-nobel/biographical/will/index.html
[106] http://www.nobel.se/help/faq/nobel_laureates.html
[107] http://almaz.com/nobel/nobel.html
[108] http://www.quotationspage.com
[109] http://almaz.com/nobel/nobel.html
[110] http://www.geometry.net/nobel/curie_marie.php
[111] http://almaz.com/nobel/nobel.html
[112] http://www.nobel.se/peace/laureates/1905/suttner-bio.html
[113] http://www.kirjasto.sci.fi/lagerlof.htm
[114] http://www.kirjasto.sci.fi/deledda.htm
[115] http://www.kirjasto.sci.fi/undset.htm
[116] http://www.nobel.se/peace/laureates/1931/addams-bio.html
[117] http://www.nobel.se/chemistry/laureates/1935/joliot-curie-bio.html)
[118] http://www.english.upenn.edu/Projects/Buck/biography.html
[119] http://www.nobel.se/literature/laureates/1945/mistral-bio.html
[120] http://www.nobel.se/peace/laureates/1946/balch-bio.html
[121] http://almaz.com/nobel/nobel.html
[122] http://www.us-israel.org/jsource/biography/cori.html
[123] http://almaz.com/nobel/nobel.html
[124] http://hum.amu.edu.pl/~zbzw/ph/sci/mgm.htm
[125] http://www.physics.ucla.edu/~moszkows/mgm/rgsmgm4.htm
[126] http://hum.amu.edu.pl/~zbzw/ph/sci/mgm.htm
[127] http://almaz.com/nobel/nobel.html
[128] http://inventors.about.com/gi/dynamic/offsite.htm?site=http://www.sdsc.edu/Science Women/hodgkin.html
[129] http://almaz.com/nobel/nobel.html
[130] http://inventors.about.com/gi/dynamic/offsite.htm?site=http://www.sdsc.edu/Science Women/hodgkin.html
[131] http://www.nobel.se/literature/laureates/1966/sachs-autobio.html
[132] http://www.nobel.se/literature/laureates/1966/sachs-autobio.html
[133] http://www.kirjasto.sci.fi/nsachs.htm
[134] http://almaz.com/nobel/nobel.html
[135] http://www.nobel.se/peace/laureates/1976/williams-cv.html
[136] http://infoplease.kids.lycos.com/ce6/people/A0852323.html
[137] http://provost.syr.edu/lectures/williams.asp.
[138] http://www.nobel.se/peace/laureates/1976/williams-cv.html
[139] http://www.peacepeople.com/MaireadByJohnDear.htm
[140] http://almaz.com/nobel/nobel.html
[141] http://www.nobel.se/medicine/laureates/1977/yalow-autobio.html
[142] http://almaz.com/nobel/nobel.html
[143] http://www.nobel.se/peace/laureates/1979/teresa-bio.html

[144] http://almaz.com/nobel/nobel.html
[145] http://www.nobel.se/peace/laureates/1979/teresa-bio.html
[146] http://www.nobel.se/peace/laureates/1982/myrdal-bio.html
[147] http://www.sipri.se/
[148] http://www.nobel.se/peace/laureates/1982/myrdal-bio.html
[149] http://www.malaspina.com/site/person_823.asp
[150] http://www.astr.ua.edu/4000WS/MCCLINTOCK.html
[151] http://www.astr.ua.edu/4000WS/MCCLINTOCK.html
[152] http://www.hup.harvard.edu/reviews/COMTAN_R.html
[153] http://www.malaspina.com/site/person_823.asp
[154] http://www.astr.ua.edu/4000WS/MCCLINTOCK.html
[155] http://almaz.com/nobel/nobel.html
[156] http://www.nobel.se/medicine/laureates/1986/levi-montalcini-autobio.html
[157] http://www.immaculata.edu/bioinformatics/thoang/woman_in_science.htm
[158] http://www.nobel.se/medicine/laureates/1986/levi-montalcini-autobio.html
[159] http://www.immaculata.edu/bioinformatics/thoang/woman_in_science.htm
[160] http://almaz.com/nobel/nobel.html
[161] http://search.biography.com/print_record.pl?id=14554
[162] http://jchemed.chem.wisc.edu/JCEWWW/Features/eChemists/Bios/Elion.html
[163] http://www.nobel.se/peace/laureates/1991/kyi-bio.html
[164] http://www.nobel.se/peace/laureates/1991/kyi-bio.html
[165] http://www.ibiblio.org/freeburma/photos/phyo/suukyi.html
[166] http://www.nobel.se/peace/laureates/1991/kyi-bio.html
[167] http://www.nobel.se/literature/laureates/1991/gordimer-bio.html
[168] http://www.scholars.nus.edu.sg/post/sa/gordimer/gordimerbio.html
[169] http://www.nobel.se/peace/laureates/1992/tum-bio.html
[170] http://www.nobel.se/peace/laureates/1992/tum-bio.html
[171] http://www.nobel.se/literature/laureates/1993/morrison-cv.html
[172] http://www.oprah.com/obc/pastbooks/toni_morrison/
[173] http://www.nobel.se/literature/laureates/1993/morrison-cv.html
[174] http://www.oprah.com/obc/pastbooks/toni_morrison/
[175] http://almaz.com/nobel/nobel.html
[176] http://www.nobel.se/medicine/laureates/1995/nusslein-volhard-autobio.html
[177] http://www.nobel.se/medicine/laureates/1995/nusslein-volhard-autobio.html
[178] http://www.nobel.se/medicine/laureates/1995/nusslein-volhard-autobio.html
[179] http://www.polishworld.com/wsz/
[180] http://www.cnn.com/WORLD/9610/03/nobel/index.html
[181] http://www.cnn.com/WORLD/9610/03/nobel/index.html
[182] http://www.polishworld.com/wsz/
[183] http://www.nobel.se/peace/laureates/1997/williams-cv.html
[184] http://www.icbl.org/amb/williams/bio.html
[185] http://www.nobel.se/peace/laureates/1997/williams-cv.html
[186] http://www.icbl.org/amb/williams/bio.html
[187] http://www.icbl.org/amb/williams/bio.html
[188] http://womenshistory.about.com/gi/dynamic/offsite.htm?site=http%3A%2F%2Fww
w.galegroup.com%2Ffree_resources%2Fwhm%2Fbio%2Fdidriksonzaharias_b.htm
[189] http://espn.go.com/page2/s/list/moments/uswomen.html
[190] http://womenshistory.about.com/gi/dynamic/offsite.htm?site=http%3A%2F%2Fww
w.galegroup.com%2Ffree_resources%2Fwhm%2Fbio%2Fdidriksonzaharias_b.htm
[191] http://www.infoplease.com/ipsa/A0114502.html

The Age of the Female II: Heroines of the Shift

[192] http://womenshistory.about.com/gi/dynamic/offsite.htm?site=http%3A%2F%2Fww
w.xrefer.com%2Fentry%2F173584

[193] http://www.infoplease.com/ipsa/A0114502.html

[194] http://womenshistory.about.com/gi/dynamic/offsite.htm?site=http%3A%2F%2Fww
w.galegroup.com%2Ffree_resources%2Fwhm%2Fbio%2Fdidriksonzaharias_b.htm

[195] http://espn.go.com/page2/s/list/moments/uswomen.html

[196] http://womenshistory.about.com/gi/dynamic/offsite.htm?site=http%3A%2F%2Fww
w.galegroup.com%2Ffree_resources%2Fwhm%2Fbio%2Fdidriksonzaharias_b.htm

[197] http://womenshistory.about.com/gi/dynamic/offsite.htm?site=http%3A%2F%2Fww
w.xrefer.com%2Fentry%2F173584

[198] http://sportsillustrated.cnn.com/siforwomen/top_100/4/

[199] http://womenshistory.about.com/library/bio/blbio_sonja_henie.htm

[200] http://sportsillustrated.cnn.com/siforwomen/top_100/4/

[201] http://www.brainyquote.com/quotes/quotes/b/q121917.html

[202] http://sportsillustrated.cnn.com/siforwomen/top_100/3/

[203] http://www.wic.org/bio/bking.htm

[204] http://www.usopen.org/about/all-time.html

[205] http://www.wslegends.com/speakers_billie_jean_king.htm

[206] http://www.wslegends.com/speakers_billie_jean_king.htm

[207] http://www.cybernation.com/victory/quotations/authors/quotes_rudolph_wilma.html

[208] http://sportsillustrated.cnn.com/siforwomen/top_100/8/

[209] http://espn.go.com/sportscentury/features/00016444.html

[210] http://www.lkwdpl.org/wihohio/rudo-wil.htm

[211] http://espn.go.com/sportscentury/features/00016444.html

[212] http://www.lkwdpl.org/wihohio/rudo-wil.htm

[213] http://belta.press.net.by/archive_eng/99/12/02/3.htm

[214] http://www.us-israel.org/jsource/Terrorism/munich.html

[215] http://sportsillustrated.cnn.com/siforwomen/top_100/18/

[216] http://www.olgakorbut.com/

[217] http://www.olgakorbut.com/

[218] http://www.infoplease.com/ipsa/A0109363.html

[219] http://www.olgakorbut.com/

[220] http://quotesland.com/view.php?do=view&full_quotes=yes&author_id=3146

[221] http://www.infoplease.com/ipsa/A0109075.html

[222] http://sportsillustrated.cnn.com/siforwomen/top_100/10/

[223] http://www.infoplease.com/ipsa/A0114780.html

[224] http://sportsillustrated.cnn.com/siforwomen/top_100/10/

[225] http://www.hickoksports.com/biograph/caulkint.shtml

[226] http://www.cyber
nation.com/victory/quotations/authors/quotes_comaneci_nadia.html

[227] http://sportsillustrated.cnn.com/siforwomen/top_100/9/

[228] http://www.gymn-forum.com/bios/comaneci.html

[229] http://www.hickoksports.com/history/olgymnas.shtml

[230] http://www.gymn-forum.com/bios/comaneci.html

[231] http://www.gymn-forum.com/results/UniGame/wuni-81aa_1.html

[232] http://sportsillustrated.cnn.com/siforwomen/top_100/9/

[233] http://sportsillustrated.cnn.com/siforwomen/top_100/23/

[234] http://sportsillustrated.cnn.com/siforwomen/top_100/23/

[235] http://horsesetcinc.com/JKFanClub.htm

[236] http://sportsillustrated.cnn.com/siforwomen/top_100/23/

[237] http://horsesetcinc.com/JKFanClub.htm
[238] http://sportsillustrated.cnn.com/siforwomen/top_100/23/
[239] http://womenshistory.about.com/library/qu/blqukron.htm
[240] http://sportsillustrated.cnn.com/siforwomen/top_100/7/
[241] http://womenshistory.about.com/gi/dynamic/offsite.htm?site=http://www.britannica.com/eb/article%3Feu=137570%26tocid=0
[242] http://sportsillustrated.cnn.com/siforwomen/top_100/7/
[243] http://sportsillustrated.cnn.com/siforwomen/top_100/7/
[244] http://www.hwwilson.com/currentbio/speedsk.html
[245] http://www.sportsstarsusa.com/olympians/blair_bonnie.html
[246] http://sportsillustrated.cnn.com/siforwomen/top_100/15/
[247] http://tracy_prinze.tripod.com/theentertainerswelove/id33.html
[248] http://tracy_prinze.tripod.com/theentertainerswelove/id33.html
[249] http://www.hickoksports.com/quotes/quoteb01.shtml#benoitjoan
[250] http://www.hickoksports.com/biograph/benoitjo.shtml
[251] http://www.olympics.org.uk/olympicmovement/olympicissueswoman.asp
[252] http://www.hickoksports.com/biograph/benoitjo.shtml
[253] http://students.juniata.edu/steinal7/quote.htm
[254] http://www.spinabifida.org/Spina%20Bifida.htm
[255] http://sportsillustrated.cnn.com/siforwomen/top_100/25/
[256] http://www.jeandriscoll.com/biography.htm
[257] http://www.jeandriscoll.com/biography.htm
[258] http://sportsillustrated.cnn.com/siforwomen/top_100/5/
[259] http://sportsillustrated.cnn.com/siforwomen/top_100/5/
[260] http://www.altosport.com/g/steffi-graf/
[261] http://search.biography.com/print_record.pl?id=5258
[262] http://sportsillustrated.cnn.com/siforwomen/top_100/14/
[263] http://search.biography.com/print_record.pl?id=5258
[264] http://search.biography.com/print_record.pl?id=5258
[265] http://www.cyber-nation.com/victory/quotations/authors/quotes_fleming_peggy.html
[266] http://www.peggyfleming.net/story.html
[267] http://www.hickoksports.com/biograph/flemingpeg.shtml
[268] http://www.peggyfleming.net/story.html
[269] http://sportsillustrated.cnn.com/siforwomen/top_100/19/
[270] http://www.hickoksports.com/biograph/flemingpeg.shtml
[271] http://www.peggyfleming.net/story.html
[272] http://ca.geocities.com/womeninnascar/quotes.html
[273] http://www.si.edu/about/mission.htm
[274] http://www.si.edu/about/mission.htm
[275] http://www.janetguthrie.com/
[276] http://www.hickoksports.com/biograph/guthriejan.shtml
[277] http://www.janetguthrie.com/
[278] http://www.thinkexist.com/english/Author/x/Author_4652_1.htm
[279] http://www.ussoccer.com/bio/bio.sps?iBiographyId=1080
[280] http://www.womensoccer.com/biogs/hamm.html
[281] http://www.womensoccer.com/biogs/hamm.html
[282] http://espn.go.com/page2/s/list/moments/uswomen.html
[283] http://www.cyber-nation.com/victory/quotations/authors/quotes_lopez_nancy.html
[284] http://www.latinosportslegends.com/Lopez_Nancy-bio.htm

The Age of the Female II: Heroines of the Shift

285 http://sportsillustrated.cnn.com/siforwomen/top_100/13/

286 http://nh.essortment.com/nancylopezbiog_rego.htm

287 http://www.latinosportslegends.com/Lopez_Nancy-bio.htm

288 http://www.cs.colorado.edu/VDC/classSpring2002/ProjectFiles/Sojourner/nancy.html

289 http://greenlees.digitalrice.com/quotes.htm

290 http://sportsillustrated.cnn.com/tennis/2001/us_open/grandslam_winners/

291 http://sportsillustrated.cnn.com/siforwomen/top_100/16/

292 http://www.auspost.com.au/BCP/0,1080,CH3022%257EMO19,00.html

293 http://www.famouscreativewomen.com/one/2108.htm

294 http://www.runnersworld.com/home/0,1300,1-141-142-1113,00.html

295 http://womenshistory.about.com/gi/dynamic/offsite.htm?site=http%3A%2F%2Fww
w.sacbee.com%2Fnews%2Fprojects%2Fpeople_of_century%2Fsports%2Fgriffith.html
and http://news.bbc.co.uk/1/hi/sport/177433.stm

296 http://womenshistory.about.com/gi/dynamic/offsite.htm?site=http%3A%2F%2Fsport
sillustrated.cnn.com%2Folympics%2Ffeatures%2Fjoyner%2Fflojo_noden.html

297 http://www.brainyquote.com/quotes/quotes/j/q140477.html

298 http://www.cyber-
nation.com/victory/quotations/authors/quotes_kersee_jackiejoyner.html

299 http://www.sacbee.com/static/archive/news/projects/people_of_century/sports/kersee
.html

300 http://www.usatoday.com/sports/olympics/otf/otfmsc21.htm

301 http://www.sacbee.com/static/archive/news/projects/people_of_century/sports/kersee
.html

302 http://sportsillustrated.cnn.com/siforwomen/top_100/1/

303 http://www.sacbee.com/static/archive/news/projects/people_of_century/sports/kersee
.html

304 http://www.sacbee.com/static/archive/news/projects/people_of_century/sports/kersee
.html.

305 http://sportsillustrated.cnn.com/siforwomen/top_100/1/

306 http://www.kirjasto.sci.fi/annefran.htm

307 http://www.kirjasto.sci.fi/annefran.htm

308 http://www.kirjasto.sci.fi/annefran.htm

309 http://www.kirjasto.sci.fi/annefran.htm

310 http://tinpan.fortunecity.com/haight/282/annebio.html

311 http://www.kirjasto.sci.fi/annefran.htm

312 http://www.allsands.com/History/People/annefrankbiogr_ft_gn.htm

313 http://www.kirjasto.sci.fi/annefran.htm

314 http://www.distinguishedwomen.com/biographies/frank.html

315 http://www.cyber-
nation.com/victory/quotations/authors/quotes_walters_barbara.html

316 http://www.biography.com/tv/listings/walters_b.html

317 http://www.biography.com/tv/listings/walters_b.html

318 http://ilil.essortment.com/barbarawalters_otq.htm

319 http://abcnews.go.com/onair/2020/walters_barbara_bio.html

320 http://www.brainyquote.com/quotes/authors/b/a125595.html

321 http://abcnews.go.com/onair/2020/walters_barbara_bio.html

322 http://www.brainyquote.com/quotes/quotes/e/q126918.html

323 http://www.quotationspage.com/quotes/Eleanor_Roosevelt

324 http://www.wic.org/bio/roosevel.htm

325 http://www.whitehouse.gov/history/firstladies/ar32.html

King

[326] http://www.distinguishedwomen.com/biographies/roosevel.html
[327] http://www.whitehouse.gov/history/firstladies/ar32.html
[328] http://www.wic.org/bio/roosevel.htm
[329] http://www.brainyquote.com/quotes/quotes/e/q126918.html
[330] http://www.udhr.org/history/Biographies/bioer.htm
[331] http://www.udhr.org/history/Biographies/bioer.htm
[332] http://www.un.org/Overview/rights.html
[333] http://www.quotationspage.com/quotes/Elisabeth_Kubler-Ross/
[334] http://abcnews.go.com/sections/living/DailyNews/kublerross.html
[335] http://www.elisabethkublerross.com/
[336] http://www.elisabethkublerross.com/
[337] http://abcnews.go.com/sections/living/DailyNews/kublerross.html
[338] http://www.elisabethkublerross.com/
[339] http://www.elisabethkublerross.com/
[340] http://www.brainyquote.com/quotes/authors/g/a127816.html
[341] http://www.distinguishedwomen.com/biographies/meir.html
[342] http://womenshistory.about.com/gi/dynamic/offsite.htm?site=http://www.israel%2D
mfa.gov.il/mfa/go.asp%3FMFAH00g40
[343] http://www.distinguishedwomen.com/biographies/meir.html
[344] http://www.wic.org/bio/gmeir.htm
[345] http://www.distinguishedwomen.com/biographies/meir.html
[346] http://womenshistory.about.com/library/weekly/aa010128a.htm
[347] http://www.wic.org/bio/gmeir.htm
[348] http://www.us-israel.org/jsource/History/73_War.html
[349] http://www.us-israel.org/jsource/biography/meir.html
[350] http://www.wic.org/bio/gmeir.htm
[351] http://www.brainyquote.com/quotes/quotes/h/q101340.html
[352] http://www.quotationspage.com/quotes/Helen_Keller/11
[353] http://www.afb.org/info_document_view.asp?documentid=1351
[354] http://www.afb.org/info_document_view.asp?documentid=1351
[355] http://www.afb.org/info_document_view.asp?documentid=1351
[356] http://www.mr-moody.com/goldenboy/1955.htm
[357] http://www.afb.org/info_document_view.asp?documentid=1351
[358] http://womenshistory.about.com/library/qu/blqugand.htm
[359] http://www.worldwatch.org/alerts/990813.html
[360] http://www.ethnologue.com/show_country.asp?name=India
[361] http://search.biography.com/print_record.pl?id=5147
[362] http://womenshistory.about.com/gi/dynamic/offsite.htm?site=http%3A%2F%2Fww
w.xrefer.com%2Fentry%2F172628
[363] http://womenshistory.about.com/gi/dynamic/offsite.htm?site=http%3A%2F%2Fww
w.xrefer.com%2Fentry%2F172628
[364] http://www.sscnet.ucla.edu/southasia/History/Independent/Indira.html
[365] http://www.distinguishedwomen.com/biographies/gandhi.html
[366] http://www.sscnet.ucla.edu/southasia/History/Independent/Indira.html
[367] http://www.sscnet.ucla.edu/southasia/History/Independent/Indira.html
[368] http://www.distinguishedwomen.com/biographies/gandhi.html
[369] http://womenshistory.about.com/library/qu/blquonas.htm
[370] http://www.bena.com/lucidcafe/library/96jul/jackie.html
[371] http://www.whitehouse.gov/history/firstladies/jk35.html
[372] http://www.whitehouse.gov/history/firstladies/jk35.html

The Age of the Female II: Heroines of the Shift

[373] http://bellaonline.com/articles/art8422.asp
[374] http://fl.essortment.com/lucilleballbi_rtkn.htm

[375] http://fl.essortment.com/lucilleballbi_rtkn.htm
[376] http://fl.essortment.com/lucilleballbi_rtkn.htm
[377] http://fl.essortment.com/lucilleballbi_rtkn.htm
[378] http://fl.essortment.com/lucilleballbi_rtkn.htm
[379] http://fl.essortment.com/lucilleballbi_rtkn.htm
[380] http://womenshistory.about.com/library/qu/blqumead.htm
[381] http://www.distinguishedwomen.com/biographies/mead.html
[382] http://www.mead2001.org/Biography.htm.
[383] http://www.anthro.mankato.msus.edu/information/biography/klmno/mead_margaret.html
[384] http://www.mead2001.org/Biography.htm
[385] http://www.distinguishedwomen.com/biographies/mead.html
[386] http://www.mead2001.org/Biography.htm
[387] http://www.wic.org/bio/mmead.htm
[388] http://www.mead2001.org/Biography.htm
[389] http://www.wic.org/bio/mmead.htm
[390] http://www.wic.org/bio/mmead.htm
[391] http://www.mead2001.org/Biography.htm
[392] http://emuseum.mnsu.edu/information/biography/klmno/mead_margaret.html
[393] http://www.mead2001.org/Biography.htm
[394] http://www.brainyquote.com/quotes/quotes/m/q114273.html
[395] http://www.distinguishedwomen.com/biographies/thatcher.html
[396] http://www.bbc.co.uk/history/state/monarchs_leaders/thatcher.shtml
[397] http://www.britannia.com/gov/primes/prime56.html
[398] http://www.distinguishedwomen.com/biographies/thatcher.html
[399] http://www.bbc.co.uk/history/state/monarchs_leaders/thatcher.shtml
[400] http://womenshistory.about.com/gi/dynamic/offsite.htm?site=http://www.time.com/time/time100/leaders/profile/thatcher.html
[401] http://www.distinguishedwomen.com/biographies/thatcher.html
[402] http://www.bbc.co.uk/history/state/monarchs_leaders/thatcher.shtml
[403] http://www.bbc.co.uk/history/state/monarchs_leaders/thatcher.shtml
[404] http://www.britannia.com/gov/primes/prime56.html
[405] http://www.dsptech.demon.co.uk/marilyn/
[406] http://www.dsptech.demon.co.uk/marilyn/
[407] http://ellensplace.net/mmbio3.html
[408] http://www.memorablequotations.com/monroe.htm
[409] http://www.memorablequotations.com/monroe.htm
[410] http://ellensplace.net/mmbio3.html
[411] http://www.bombshells.com/gallery/monroe/monroe_facts.shtml
[412] http://ellensplace.net/mmbio3.html
[413] http://www.marilynmonroe.com/about/bio.html
[414] http://www.marilynmonroe.com/about/bio.html
[415] http://www.marilynmonroe.com/about/bio.html
[416] http://www.bombshells.com/gallery/monroe/monroe_facts.shtml
[417] http://www.memorablequotations.com/monroe.htm
[418] http://www.bombshells.com/gallery/monroe/monroe_facts.shtml
[419] http://www.brainyquote.com/quotes/authors/o/a130556.html

[420] http://www.angelfire.com/ne/lliegirls/winfrey.html
[421] http://www.achievement.org/autodoc/page/win0bio-1
[422] http://ksks.essortment.com/oprahwinfrey_rkcr.htm
[423] http://www.oprah.com/about/press/about_press_bio.jhtml
[424] http://search.eb.com/blackhistory/micro/721/87.html
[425] http://www.oprah.com/about/press/about_press_bio.jhtml
[426] http://www.oprah.com/about/press/about_press_bio.jhtml
[427] http://www.oprah.com/about/press/about_press_bio.jhtml
[428] http://www.achievement.org/autodoc/page/win0bio-1
[429] http://www.oprah.com/about/press/about_press_bio.jhtml
[430]
[431] http://www.brainyquote.com/quotes/authors/o/a130556.html
[432] http://www.oprah.com/about/press/about_press_bio.jhtml
[433] http://www.brainyquote.com/quotes/authors/s/a131529.html
[434] http://creativequotations.com/one/1196.htm
[435] http://usgovinfo.about.com/blcthistory.htm
[436] http://www.supremecourthistory.org/justice/o'connor.htm
[437] http://www.supremecourthistory.org/justice/o'connor.htm
[438] http://www.supremecourthistory.org/justice/o'connor.htm

To order books, go to

www.RichardKing.Net

Contact

Richard Andrew King

PO Box 3621

Laguna Hills, CA 92654

www.RichardKing.net

King